COUNTRY LIVING

THE ★ FARM CHICKS

IN THE *Kitchen*

TERI EDWARDS ★ **SERENA THOMPSON**

HEARST BOOKS

A division of Sterling Publishing Co., Inc.

New York / London

www.sterlingpublishing.com

PHOTOGRAPHY CREDITS

Justin Bernhaut: page 11 top right.

Joseph de Leo: 110.

Thayer Allyson Gowdy: 6, 7 right, 29, 74 left, 75 right, 76, 114, 116, 120, 121, 122, 127, 128, 136 left, 137 right.

John Granen: 2, 4, 8 bottom left and top, 17 bottom, 28 bottom, 30, 34, 37, 41, 42, 44, 45, 47, 49, 50, 54, 58, 61, 65, 68, 70, 73, 76, 81, 86, 88, 92, 94, 96, 101, 102, 104, 125, 131, 140.

Debra McClinton: 5, 10, 11 top left and top middle, 12, 18, 24, 59, 89, 97, 136 right, 137 left, opposite page 144.

Tina Rupp: 80.

Charles Schiller: 98.

Jeff Schindler, www.schindlerphotography.com: 27 bottom, 36 left.

Ann Stratton: 82.

Robin Stubbert: 83.

All other photos courtesy of the authors.

Magner Sanborn created the Farm Chicks graphics on pages 1, 124, 141, and the floral motif on the recipe pages and case cover.

Michael Miller Fabrics, designed by **Sandi Henderson,** appear in the photos on pages 42, 65, 87, 104, and 133.

This book was previously published as a hardcover under the title *The Farm Chicks in the Kitchen.*

Project Editor: **Carol Spier**
Design: **woolypear**

Library of Congress Cataloging-in-Publication Data is available.

10 9 8 7 6 5 4 3 2 1

Published by Hearst Books
A Division of Sterling Publishing Co., Inc.
387 Park Avenue South, New York, NY 10016

The Farm Chicks is a trademark of The Farm Chicks, Inc.
Country Living is a registered trademark of Hearst Communications, Inc.

www.countryliving.com

For information about custom editions, special sales, premium and corporate purchases, please contact Sterling Special Sales Department at 800-805-5489 or specialsales@sterlingpublishing.com.

Distributed in Canada by Sterling Publishing
c/o Canadian Manda Group, 165 Dufferin Street
Toronto, Ontario, Canada M6K 3H6

Distributed in Australia by Capricorn Link (Australia) Pty. Ltd.
P.O. Box 704, Windsor, NSW 2756 Australia

Manufactured in China

Sterling ISBN 978-1-58816-866-5

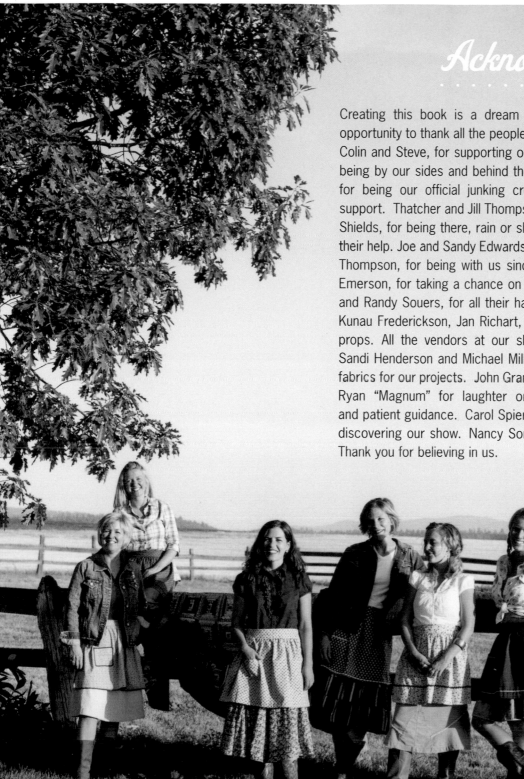

Acknowledgments

Creating this book is a dream come true for us. We want to take this opportunity to thank all the people who helped to turn our dream into a reality: Colin and Steve, for supporting our dreams. Kate, Allie, and Emil, for always being by our sides and behind the scenes. Cody, Micah, Lucas, and Bongo, for being our official junking crew. Heather, for her artwork and sisterly support. Thatcher and Jill Thompson, for their generosity. Chuck and Dolores Shields, for being there, rain or shine. Pete and Mary Jane Thompson, for all their help. Joe and Sandy Edwards, for doing all the hard lifting. Lyle and Elaine Thompson, for being with us since the beginning. Nancy Bridges and Heidi Emerson, for taking a chance on us when we were just getting started. Lisa and Randy Souers, for all their hard work and creativity. Sally Barlow, Nancy Kunau Frederickson, Jan Richart, and Celeste Shaw, for loaning us so many props. All the vendors at our show, for creating such an amazing event. Sandi Henderson and Michael Miller Fabrics, for supplying so many beautiful fabrics for our projects. John Granen, for making everything look beautiful and Ryan "Magnum" for laughter on the set. Marisa Bulzone, for her kind and patient guidance. Carol Spier, for her wonderful work. Monica Willis, for discovering our show. Nancy Soriano, for her support and encouragement. Thank you for believing in us.

Contents

Serena and Teri with a promotional package ready to send to *Country Living*.

FOREWORD

We travel a fair amount around the country each year, and it's something we really enjoy. Being out and about enables us to meet creative, entrepreneurial women on their home turf, where we can enjoy and fully appreciate their talents. In the spring of 2005, several colleagues from *Country Living* checked out The Farm Chicks Antique Show, which at that time was held in a small, rural town not far from Spokane, Washington. We'd been intrigued by the promotional materials sent to us by the show's producers, Teri Edwards and Serena Thompson, and charmed by their motto: Live Well, Laugh Often, Junk Much.

What fun we had. Teri and Serena are firm friends and smart business partners who named themselves The Farm Chicks when they held their first small sale in a neighbor's yard. Now a much larger enterprise, The Farm Chicks Antique Show is as fun and family friendly as they are, with lots of antiques dealers and farmer's-market vendors, bluegrass music, great country food, and kids—the next generation of collectors—everywhere. We certainly lived well, laughed a lot, and junked to our hearts content while visiting the show. And as we came to know Teri and Serena, we learned they are adept cooks who turn out exquisite pies and all manner of delicious country eats, plus they have a distinctive sense of style that we find irresistible. We were excited about introducing them to the *Country Living* readers.

As early as that first meeting, we were talking about ways The Farm Chicks could share their love of family, good food, and giving found treasures new life with people who couldn't visit the show (or for whom a once-a-year event simply wasn't enough). We tossed around the idea of a cookbook filled with their favorite recipes and thought it would be great to include some of their charming junk makeovers and other homemade accessories. As we talked, we knew we wanted the book to be something more. We were fascinated by the story of two seemingly ordinary women, married with children, who didn't work outside their homes and had no business experience and no special resources, who followed their hearts and their natural talents to become successful entrepreneurs. Please meet The Farm Chicks—may they inspire you to tie on an apron and cook well, junk much, make your homes happy places, enjoy your neighbors, and laugh often.

The editors of *Country Living*

TERI'S STORY

I am the fourth of six children, born and raised in the Yakima Valley of Washington State. Mom had five babies in eight years and then eight years later along came my baby brother, Andy. She fondly refers to him as "the caboose." Dad worked long, hard hours at a cement company while Mom had the challenge of stretching his paycheck to meet the needs of a family of eight. We were lucky to live in a farming community where fruits and vegetables were plentiful. There was a lot of canning and freezing to help get us through the year. My favorite was Mom's canned cherries with the yummy sweet juice. We'd eat them by the bowlful!

We lived in a series of farmhouses, rented from local farmers who would also provide after-school and summer jobs for all of us kids. Jobs usually passed from one sibling to the next as we got older and could handle more responsibility. Like any kid, my favorite jobs were those that had anything to do with animals and I could hardly wait to be "promoted" to herding. It was common practice to use geese to weed the mint fields. My sister Kathy was in charge of the geese, but when she became too busy with other responsibilities, it was finally my turn to take charge of them!

EAGER TO HELP

In the early evening after dinner, I would head out to the fields to round up the flock. They would be fed and penned up for safekeeping until the next morning, when they would head out for another day of munching on weeds. When they were all in the pen, I would count them to make sure they were all there. If not, off I would go on the search for those few that always seemed to find their way through the fence to freedom. I remember tagging along with Kathy and quizzing her about them, trying to prepare myself for the day that I would be in

THE **FARM CHICKS' STORY**

Teri was preparing dinner when she received a call from Sister Kathleen about a woman who was new to the area and had begun attending their Catholic church. She wanted to share in the faith of her future husband and family. Sister Kathleen asked Teri if she would be interested in volunteering as a sponsor for the woman over the coming year. Although Teri wanted to help, she decided it would be too large a commitment and hard on her young family. She declined. But she couldn't shake the feeling that she shouldn't have said no and after much prayer and discussion with her husband, decided that she would agree to be the woman's sponsor. That woman was me, Serena.

My friend Teri isn't my sister but she might as well be. We share common interests, dreams, love of family, and a desire to do good that was taught to us as children. That desire was alive one day as I was unloading a filthy old metal tool box amongst a load of old goods from the back of a stranger's truck. "I love old junk," I said. "Well if you like that, you should come check out my old cabin on the mountain," my neighbor Clayton replied.

The load that day was one of hundreds I'd received while organizing a fundraiser for a wonderful man, Paul, who was a volunteer firefighter with my husband. He had been diagnosed with a form of cancer, and we wanted to help. Paul was a good man, one who'd light up a room and make you feel happy with a simple smile. He was a neighbor in the true sense of the word, always willing to help anyone who was in need, and never had a negative thing to say about anyone. I'd suggested holding a rummage sale as a way for us, as neighbors and friends, to show our love for a good man, and hoped it would help with Paul's medical expenses, and quite possibly, those of his funeral. The sale raised thousands of dollars and Paul was deeply touched by the outpouring of support from the community. Sadly, Paul lost his battle with cancer shortly thereafter.

Many months went by and I saw Clayton again. He made another offer for me to go through the old cabin he had inherited from his Aunt Ruby—a strong and independent

❋ *Breakfast* ❋

cinnamon rolls

MAKES 12 ROLLS	
WORKING TIME 40 MINUTES	
TOTAL TIME 3 HOURS	

On their birthdays, my children are allowed to choose all the meals. This recipe is almost always the requested breakfast treat. To make it easier, I add the ingredients into my bread machine on the dough cycle. If you don't have a bread machine, just follow the steps described below. ~Serena Shown on page 30.

. . . .

1 cup milk	4 cups all-purpose flour
2¼ teaspoons active dry yeast	½ teaspoon salt
½ cup granulated sugar	1 cup packed brown sugar
½ cup unsalted butter (1 stick), softened	2 teaspoons ground cinnamon
2 large eggs	Cream Cheese Icing (recipe follows)

Make the dough: Heat the milk in a small saucepan over low heat or in a microwave until it is warm, not hot (105°F to 115°F). Add it to a large mixing bowl. Sprinkle the yeast on top and let it sit until dissolved—approximately 3 minutes. Meanwhile, melt ¼ cup butter in a small saucepan over low heat or in a microwave. Whisk the granulated sugar, eggs, and melted butter into the milk mixture. Stir in the flour and salt with a wooden spoon, mixing until the ingredients are well combined. Cover the bowl with plastic wrap or a clean damp kitchen towel and let rest for 30 minutes.

Proof the dough: Turn the dough out onto a lightly floured surface and knead for 3 minutes. Lightly oil another large bowl. Place the dough in the bowl; turn to coat with oil. Cover the bowl with plastic wrap and let the dough rise in warm, draft-free area until doubled in volume—30 to 40 minutes.

Make the filling and Cream Cheese Icing: While the dough is resting, mix the brown sugar and cinnamon in a small bowl for the filling and set aside. Prepare the Cream Cheese Icing and set it aside.

Form the rolls: Butter a jelly-roll pan. Once the dough has risen, punch it down; then transfer it to a lightly floured surface and roll it into a 15- by 20-inch rectangle. Spread the remaining $1/4$ cup butter evenly over the dough using a spatula and sprinkle with the brown sugar and cinnamon mixture. Starting at 1 long side, roll up the dough jelly-roll style, forming a log. Pinch the seam and ends to seal. Use a serrated knife to cut the log crosswise into 12 equal sections. Arrange the rolls about 1-inch apart, spiral side up, in the prepared pan. Cover with parchment paper and a kitchen towel and let rise until doubled in size—about 1 hour. After 45 minutes, heat the oven to 375°F.

Bake the rolls: Once the rolls have risen, uncover them and bake until light golden brown—12 to15 minutes. Remove from the oven and immediately invert onto a wire rack. Cool 10 minutes. Turn the rolls right side up. Spread with Cream Cheese Icing and serve warm.

Cream Cheese Icing

Beat 4 tablespoons softened butter with 2 tablespoons softened cream cheese in a medium-size bowl with an electric mixer on medium speed until well blended. Beat in $3/4$ cup confectioners' sugar and $1/2$ teaspoon vanilla extract until well blended. Cover with plastic wrap until ready to use.

Nutrition per roll—Protein: 6.6 G; Fat: 14.1 G; Carbohydrate: 67.4 G; Fiber: 1.2 G; Sodium: 131.9 MG; Cholesterol: 70 MG; Calories: 420.

2 TIPS FOR THE ROLLS

1 *To ensure the rolls rise really well, heat the oven to 150°F, warm for about 2 minutes, and then turn it off. Place the rolls in the oven for 45 minutes. Then remove them so you can heat the oven for baking.*

2 *If you'd like to bake these in the morning to serve warm and fresh but don't want to get up at the crack of dawn, you can prep them the day before, cover with plastic wrap after they've risen, refrigerate overnight, and then bake as usual the next day.*

MAGNETIC MESSAGE CENTER

We see a lot of old TV trays at yard sales and thrift stores. They come in all styles and sizes, many with vibrant colors and graphics. They must have been the old standby gift of an era past because they tend to be plentiful and are usually in great shape. You don't have to eat dinner off them to appreciate their function and style. If you find an adorable one that fits the look of your home, hang it on the wall or prop it up on a bookshelf. Plus these trays make the perfect message center for a kitchen or pantry; here's all you need to do:

SUPPLY TIP
Picture hangers and bumpers can be found in the picture hanging section of a hardware or crafts supply store.

1. Thoroughly clean the tray—front and back—with a soft cloth in warm sudsy water. Do not run the tray through the dishwasher or let it soak in water as either could damage the paint surface.

2. Lay the tray face down on a towel. On the flat area, measure to find the top center and mark with a pencil. Attach a sawtooth picture hanger at the mark; use an all-purpose glue that will bond to metal and make sure the hanger is level. We used glue that came in a gel version, making it easier to work with on such a small surface area. Allow the glue to dry.

3. Affix a self-adhesive vinyl bumper on each bottom corner. This not only protects the wall from getting scraped up, but also helps to keep the tray in place.

4. Use any magnets you like to post notes on the board. We like the retro look of the kind that have a built-in clip.

cherry breakfast swirl

MAKES 20 SERVINGS
WORKING TIME 25 MINUTES
TOTAL TIME 55 MINUTES

This is a quick-and-easy recipe that tastes as good as it looks. The cherries and almonds give it the appearance of a fancy bakery treat. We usually serve it for breakfast, but it would make a tasty dessert as well. Either way, you'll love it.

1½ cups sugar

1 cup unsalted butter
(2 sticks), softened

2 teaspoons vanilla extract

1 teaspoon almond extract

4 large eggs

3 cups all-purpose flour

1½ teaspoons baking powder

1 21-ounce can cherry pie filling

½ cup sliced almonds (about 2 ounces)

Prepare the batter: Heat the oven to 350°F. Butter a large jelly-roll pan. Cream the sugar with the butter in a large mixing bowl with an electric mixer on medium speed until fluffy. Beat in the vanilla and almond extracts and the eggs. Reduce the mixer speed to medium-low and beat in the flour and baking powder just until blended.

Bake the cake: Spread two-thirds of the batter in the prepared pan; the batter will look insufficient and will spread very thinly. Scatter spoonfuls of the cherry filling over the top and dot with tablespoonfuls of the remaining batter. Then, using the back of a spoon, flatten each little mound of batter just a bit. Sprinkle on the sliced almonds. Bake until the cake is lightly browned—28 to 30 minutes. Serve warm or at room temperature. Store in the pan, covered with plastic wrap, up to 3 days.

Nutrition per serving—Protein: 3.9 G; Fat: 11.4 G; Carbohydrate: 38.6 G; Fiber: 1 G; Sodium: 62.3 MG; Cholesterol: 66.4 MG; Calories: 272.

nancy's nutmeg coffee cake

MAKES	1 NINE-INCH SQUARE CAKE (9 SERVINGS)
WORKING TIME	25 MINUTES
TOTAL TIME	1 HOUR AND 5 MINUTES

We fell in love with this recipe when our friend Nancy served it to us at her float house in Idaho. It has a delicious bottom crust that, when served warm, just melts in your mouth.

2 cups all-purpose flour

2 cups packed light-brown sugar

½ cup unsalted butter (1 stick), cut into small pieces

1 large egg, beaten

1 cup sour cream

1 teaspoon ground nutmeg

1 teaspoon baking soda

1 cup finely chopped walnuts (about 4 ounces)

1 teaspoon ground cinnamon

Prepare the crust: Heat the oven to 350°F. Mix the flour and brown sugar in a medium-size bowl. Use a pastry blender or two knives to cut in the butter until the mixture looks like sand. Spoon half the mixture into a square 9-inch pan, evenly pressing over the bottom.

Prepare the batter: Add the egg, sour cream, nutmeg, and baking soda to the flour mixture remaining in the bowl; mix until well combined. Spoon the batter over the mixture in the pan, spreading evenly. Mix the walnuts and cinnamon in a small bowl and evenly sprinkle over the batter in the pan.

Bake the cake: Bake until the center is set—about 40 minutes. Remove from the oven and cut the warm cake into nine 3-inch squares. Serve warm (the crust will be soft), or allow to cool (the crust will be crunchy). Store, covered, in the pan up to 2 days.

Nutrition per serving—Protein: 7.9 G; Fat: 24.6 G; Carbohydrate: 72.1 G; Fiber: 1.9 G; Sodium: 177.2 MG; Cholesterol: 61.5 MG; Calories: 527.

A RECIPE GIFT

We met our friends Nancy (pictured) and Sally when they began participating in our antiques show. They are co-owners of a wonderful antiques shop in Couer d'Alene, Idaho, professional decorators, and best friends. They're extremely creative and have a real knack for taking quirky objects and mixing them into any setting. We love making this coffee cake and thinking of them each time we do.

A Pantry Affair

I love my pantry. It's not much, just a converted area in my laundry room where a big upright freezer was at one time, right next to the kitchen. My husband, Steve, put up some simple, yet sturdy, shelves there to make a little pantry. Because I have a screen door on my laundry room, the pantry is visible when I come in from the garage. Wanting it to be as cute as it is convenient, I began purchasing glass pantry jars as they went on sale. Slowly, over time, I purchased enough jars to hold items like pasta, rice, breadcrumbs, chocolate chips, nuts, and much more—things I buy in bulk or that typically come in bags and boxes. I've labeled everything and spray painted the lids red to make everything uniform and, of course more importantly, cute. Not only does the pantry help me keep things organized, but now when I walk by, I sometimes catch myself stopping to enjoy the view!

~Teri

PANTRY JAR LABELS

We created these labels from vintage fabric and wallpaper to bring a little more order and cuteness to our pantries. We covered the fabric labels with clear Con-Tact paper, making them easy to clean. Covering the wallpaper isn't necessary, as it already has a wipeable surface. We loved getting everything organized.

1. Cut the wallpaper or fabric into label shapes; we prefer rectangular. To add a little charm, cut with pinking shears.

2. If using fabric, cut two pieces of clear Con-Tact paper for each label, making them 1 inch larger in each dimension. Sandwich each fabric label between the Con-Tact paper cutouts; press together to seal. Trim the Con-Tact paper so it makes a $1/4$-inch border all around the fabric.

3. For either type of label: Use a Sharpie pen to write the name of whatever you are storing on each label. Affix the labels to jars or other storage containers with double-stick tape.

HANG THE LABEL INSTEAD

For a slight variation, punch two holes at the top of the label, thread with ribbon, and hang around the neck of the jar.

HAPPY TRAILS

Many of our days have been filled with junking excursions and road trips together with our children. These days are some of our best memories as friends and mothers.

We saw an ad in the newspaper for a big yard sale in Spokane Valley that sounded pretty good. We all piled into Serena's car and headed out. The place was loaded. Serena found a great old red metal playground swing and a huge old school chalkboard. Teri spotted an old Idaho state souvenir and our children scouted for things they thought we both would love. It was perfect.

When we got back to Serena's house, we unloaded all our goods for a show-and-tell in the living room. As the kids gathered around, we all inspected our finds. After lunch, Teri's daughters, Kate and Allie, picked up an antiques guidebook and began leafing through it. They spotted an old chicken figurine in the book and screamed. We all rushed over to take a look and believed the piece they were looking at was nearly identical to one we had seen at the sale earlier that day. It was a rare piece, making it valuable. With no hesitation whatsoever, we all piled back into the car and returned to the sale. Serena's boys chanted, "We're rich! We're rich!" the entire way and Kate and Allie seemed to be in shock over their discovery.

Luckily, the "treasure chicken" was still there. We paid and headed back to Serena's so we could com-pare it to the book. It didn't take long for us to discover that our treasure wasn't valuable and that the only similarities were that both pieces were chickens. We all laughed, a lot. That day was priceless to us and gave our children the junking bug.

At an auction later that summer, Serena's boys sat captivated as they watched a variety of goods bid upon. When a large lot of baseball cards came up for bid, Lucas's tiny little arm up shot up in the air, much to Serena's surprise. As she reached for Lucas's arm, the auctioneer paused and asked if he really wanted to bid. "Yes!" said Lucas, thinking that by simply raising his arm, he could win the cards. Although Lucas left empty handed that day, he and his brothers quickly learned how an auction really works.

Teri's girls are now grown, but Serena's boys continue to be our companions on these trips. They've all become experts in the world of junk, knowing just what they're looking for and what they can expect to pay. It's second nature to them now and we love that they can see the value in items that have been used but still have some good life ahead.

pumpkin waffles

MAKES 8 STANDARD-SIZE WAFFLES
WORKING TIME 15 MINUTES
TOTAL TIME 25 MINUTES

My son Micah loves these waffles particularly because they're pumpkin. Serve them for a warm and hearty breakfast that's sure to please! ~Serena.

. . . .

2 cups all-purpose flour

2 tablespoons sugar

4 teaspoons baking powder

1 teaspoon salt

1 teaspoon ground cinnamon

¼ teaspoon ground nutmeg

3 large eggs, separated

1¾ cups milk

½ cup butter (1 stick), melted

½ cup canned pumpkin

Vegetable oil for brushing waffle iron

Maple syrup for serving

Prepare the batter: Heat the oven to 250°F. Heat a waffle iron. Combine the flour, sugar, baking powder, salt, cinnamon, and nutmeg in a large mixing bowl. Whisk together the egg yolks, milk, butter, and pumpkin in a medium-size bowl. Add the egg mixture to the flour mixture, stirring until combined. Beat the egg whites in a small bowl until stiff and fold them into the batter.

Cook the waffles: Brush the waffle iron lightly with oil and spoon in batter (about ¼ cup per waffle), spreading quickly. Cook according to the manufacturer's instructions. Transfer waffles to a rack in the oven to keep warm and crisp. Repeat with the remaining batter. Serve hot with maple syrup.

Nutrition per waffle—Protein: 7.6 G; Fat: 16.8 G; Carbohydrate: 32.4 G; Fiber: 1.5 G; Sodium: 695.4 MG; Cholesterol: 114.8 MG; Calories: 309.

MAKES 12 FIVE-INCH
GRIDDLECAKES
WORKING TIME 10 MINUTES
TOTAL TIME 25 MINUTES

cardamom griddlecakes with maple cardamom cream

Here is a tasty alternative to the ordinary pancake—deliciously spiced with a bit of cardamom and topped with a special homemade cream.

. . . .

Maple Cardamom Cream (recipe follows)

1$\frac{1}{3}$ cups all-purpose flour

3 tablespoons confectioners' sugar

2 teaspoons baking powder

1 teaspoon ground cardamom

$\frac{1}{2}$ teaspoon baking soda

3 tablespoons unsalted butter, melted, plus additional for cooking

1$\frac{1}{4}$ cups buttermilk

1 large egg

BUTTERMILK SUBSTITUTE

If you don't have butter-milk, you can easily substitute 1$\frac{1}{4}$ cups milk mixed with 1 tablespoon plus 1 teaspoon white vinegar. Combine the milk and vinegar and let sit for 10 minutes before using.

Prepare the Maple Cardamom Cream; keep warm.

Prepare the batter: Heat the oven to 250°F. Combine the flour, sugar, baking powder, cardamom, and baking soda in a large bowl. Whisk the butter, buttermilk, and egg in a medium-size bowl until the egg is thoroughly combined. Add to the dry ingredients in the large bowl, stirring just until all ingredients are combined (the batter may still be lumpy).

Cook the griddlecakes: Heat a griddle or large skillet over medium heat. Spread a thin coating of butter over the griddle and let melt. Working in batches, drop batter by $\frac{1}{3}$ cupfuls onto the griddle, spacing a few inches apart to allow for spreading. Cook the griddlecakes until brown on the bottom and bubbles form on top—about 3 minutes. Turn each griddlecake over and continue to cook until both sides are golden brown. Transfer to a baking sheet and place in the oven to keep warm. Repeat with the remaining batter, adding more butter to griddle as needed. Serve warm with Maple Cardamom Cream.

Maple Cardamom Cream

Combine $\frac{1}{2}$ cup maple syrup, 2 tablespoons heavy cream, and $\frac{1}{8}$ teaspoon ground cardamom in a small saucepan and heat over medium-low heat, stirring occasionally, until heated through—about 7 minutes. Keep warm over very low heat until ready to serve. Makes approximately $\frac{2}{3}$ cup.

Nutrition per griddlecake with sauce—Protein: 2.9 G; Fat: 5.5 G; Carbohydrate: 23.3 G; Fiber: 0.4 G; Sodium: 179.7 MG; Cholesterol: 32.1 MG; Calories: 154.

PAINT-BY-NUMBERS TRAY

You may attach handles to each side of the tray if you like. We didn't attach handles to this one so we'd have the option of returning it to the wall, should we ever choose to.

1. Make sure your framed paint-by-number painting is sturdy enough to use as a tray. Replace the frame if necessary. Remove any hanging hardware if you are using the original frame.

2. Our painting came with a sturdy wooden backing. If your painting doesn't have a firm backing, you'll need to attach one. You can use $1/4$-inch Masonite (like Peg Board without the holes). To protect the frame, place it face down on a towel while you screw the backing to it; pre-drill holes to start the screws.

3. To keep it from scratching your table, cover the entire back of the framed painting with felt, using a hot glue gun to adhere.

4. If your framed paint-by-number painting is not protected by glass, have a piece of glass or acrylic cut to fit snugly inside the frame over the painting. (Remove the glass if you decide to hang your painting on the wall again.)

The paint-by-numbers craze was big in the 1950s and '60s. What was once looked down upon by the art world is now highly collectible. Sold as kits, these pictures were painted by the average person and required little to no artistic skill and yet, they have a kitschy beauty about them. From landscapes to animals, religious themes to ballerinas, there was a subject for everyone. Painting-by-number was a very popular hobby, with millions of kits sold each year during its peak (and it has made a comeback in the past few years, with both retro-style and contemporary images available at crafts stores). We've both found several vintage examples over the years at yard sales and thrift stores; we turned this one into a bedside tray. Make yours into a tray or just hang it on the wall and think of the Sunday hobbyist who painted it years ago. These paintings are a piece of Americana.

apple puff pancake

MAKES 1 NINE-INCH ROUND PANCAKE
(8 SERVINGS)

WORKING TIME 15 MINUTES

TOTAL TIME 35 MINUTES

We love this old-fashioned recipe, which is really simple and goes well with our Golden Potato Bake (page 53). The flavor is similar to an apple pie, just in puffy pancake form. When drizzled with maple syrup, this pancake is impossible to resist.

. . . .

¼ cup unsalted butter (½ stick)

¼ cup packed brown sugar

1 teaspoon ground cinnamon

1 apple, peeled, cored, and thinly sliced

5 large eggs

½ cup milk

½ cup all-purpose flour

Dash of salt

Maple syrup or confectioners' sugar, for serving

Heat the oven to 425°F. Place the butter, brown sugar, and cinnamon in a 9-inch glass pie plate. Heat in the oven until the butter is melted and bubbly—5 minutes. Remove from the oven, stir well and mix in the apple slices. Return to the oven and bake for 2 minutes. Meanwhile, combine the eggs, milk, flour, and salt in a blender or food processor and process until frothy—1 minute. Pour over the apple mixture. Bake until the cake is puffed and the center is set—18 to 20 minutes. Serve warm with maple syrup or sprinkled with confectioners' sugar.

Nutrition per serving—Protein: 5.4 G; Fat: 9.4 G; Carbohydrate: 15.9 G; Fiber: 0.6 G; Sodium: 70.2 MG; Cholesterol: 148.8 MG; Calories: 167.

maple oat scones

MAKES 8 SCONES
WORKING TIME 30 MINUTES
TOTAL TIME 50 MINUTES

These scones are great because they're sweetened with just a bit of maple syrup, making them not too sweet, yet full of delicious maple flavor. They're the perfect accompaniment to your morning cup of coffee or tea.

. . . .

1¾ cups all-purpose flour

1½ cups old-fashioned rolled oats

2 teaspoons baking powder

10 tablespoons cold unsalted butter, cut into small pieces

⅓ cup heavy cream

¼ cup maple syrup

1 large egg, slightly beaten

½ cup chopped walnuts (about 2 ounces)

Maple Glaze (recipe follows)

THICKER OATS

Try using thick-cut rolled oats in this recipe or any recipe calling for old-fashioned rolled oats. We think they're more flavorful and chewier than the standard rolled oats or the even thinner "quick" oats.

Look for thick-cut rolled oats in the bulk section of the market, and don't confuse them with steel-cut oats, which require long cooking.

Mix the dough: Heat the oven to 425°F. Combine the flour, oats, and baking powder in a large mixing bowl. Use a pastry blender or two knives to cut the butter into the flour mixture until the butter is the size of peas. Add the cream, maple syrup, and egg; mix with a wooden spoon until well combined. Stir in the walnuts.

Bake the scones: Turn out the dough onto an unfloured work surface and form into an 8-inch round about 1-inch thick. Cut into 8 wedges and place on a baking sheet. Bake until lightly browned— 15 to 18 minutes. Remove to a wire rack to cool. Meanwhile, prepare the Maple Glaze.

Glaze the scones: Drizzle the cooled scones with Maple Glaze and serve.

Maple Glaze

Combine 1 tablespoon melted unsalted butter, 2 tablespoons maple syrup, 1 tablespoon heavy cream, and 1 cup confectioners' sugar in a small bowl and whisk together until smooth and lump free.

Nutrition per scone with glaze—Protein: 7.8 G; Fat: 26.6 G; Carbohydrate: 57.8 G; Fiber: 2.8 G; Sodium: 155 MG; Cholesterol: 84 MG; Calories: 492.

SCONE COZY

We happened upon this idea by accident, in our friend Lisa Richart's booth at our show. She had a small, circular item for sale; it was handmade from white tulle and pretty fancy. Lisa explained that it was a scone holder, which we had never heard of. And although the pattern was pretty complicated and a bit unpractical, we knew we could run with the idea. Our terry cloth version works well for keeping scones warm, much as if they were placed in a towel-covered basket, except you tuck a scone right into each of the cozy's pockets and can pass it on a plate.

What we really like about this project is that it has great gift potential. Prepare our Maple Oat Scones (opposite), place them in the cute cozy, set on a plate, and deliver to a new neighbor or send to school as a teacher-appreciation gift.

1. Cut two 11-inch diameter circles from a terry- or other thick-cloth kitchen towel.

2. Finish the raw edge of each with bias binding and, if desired, embellish with rickrack.

3. With chalk, divide one circle into six equal wedges, just as if cutting a pie. Place the marked circle on top of the second circle and sew them together along the lines.

crunchy granola

MAKES ABOUT 10 CUPS GRANOLA (20 SERVINGS)
WORKING TIME 10 MINUTES
TOTAL TIME 1 HOUR

We've adapted this recipe from our favorite granola at The Rockwood Bakery in Spokane. Serve it for breakfast at home or when camping in the woods. It's also a great treat sprinkled over yogurt.

6 cups old-fashioned rolled oats

2 cups shredded unsweetened coconut

2 cups pecan halves

1/3 cup canola oil

1/2 cup packed brown sugar

1/2 cup crunchy peanut butter

1/2 cup honey

2 teaspoons ground cinnamon

1 teaspoon vanilla extract

Mix the granola: Heat the oven to 325°F. Combine the oats, coconut, and pecans in a large mixing bowl. Combine the oil, brown sugar, peanut butter, honey, cinnamon, and vanilla in a small saucepan over medium heat and stir until smooth. Pour over the oat mixture and stir until well combined.

Bake the granola: Line a large shallow baking pan with foil. Spread the mixture in the pan. Bake until browned—about 50 minutes—stirring every 10 minutes with a large spatula. Cool in the pan on a wire rack; then stir once more. Store in an airtight container for up to 2 weeks.

Nutrition per serving—Protein: 6.1 G; Fat: 21.2 G; Carbohydrate: 33.4 G; Fiber: 5.3 G; Sodium: 35.8 MG; Cholesterol: 0 MG; Calories: 332.

BULK IS A BETTER BUY

Whenever I get a craving for a batch of our Crunchy Granola, I head right to the bulk section at our market. Since there's no expense devoted to branded packaging, items tend to be less costly and the variety just seems to be getting bigger and better. If you're short on cupboard space, you can buy only what you need for a particular recipe, or you can buy a lot to stock up the pantry. Either way, we suggest making the bulk section your friend. We love it.

~Teri

APRON APPLIQUÉ

Aprons are meant to be practical, but they can also be really adorable. If you have a plain apron that needs a little dressing up, this is the perfect project for you!

1. Trace or photocopy the patterns for the appliqué you wish to make (opposite), enlarging if you wish. Cut each piece from paper-backed fusible web (such as Wonder-Under): Remember, the paper side will be the wrong side of the finished appliqué. Fuse each piece to appropriate fabric following the directions on the fusible-web package. Cut out the shapes and remove the paper backing.

2. For the cake and cake interior pieces, trace the design lines on the patterns onto the fabric cutouts using a fabric marker or pencil. (This is easily done by holding fabric and pattern up to a window.)

3. Decide where to place the appliqué on your apron. Position the bottom cutout first (the plate on the cake pattern or the cake on the cupcake pattern.) Iron into place. Sew rickrack over the edge of the fabric cutout as shown in the photo; we used jumbo rickrack around the plate and regular rickrack around the cupcake.

4. Position the remaining cutouts on top of the first. Iron into place. Sew jumbo rickrack over the edge of the cupcake frosting. Use a satin stitch on your sewing machine to outline the edge and interior lines of the cake as shown in the photo, or if you prefer, embellish by hand with embroidery thread.

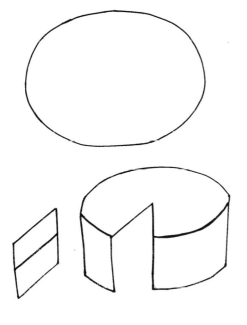

The Perfect Apron

One afternoon, on the way home from the gym, I stopped by a favorite little antiques shop of mine. After browsing a bit, I glanced at my watch and realized school would be ending soon and that I needed to leave to pick up my children. On the way out, I spotted the greatest apron of all time. It was a simple little half apron, adorned with an appliquéd 1st place blue ribbon, a bull, cow brands, and the name "Mrs. Howdy" in script across the bottom. Looking at the blue ribbon reminded me of all the baking contests I had entered as a child and the bull made me smile, as my home is filled with old framed black and whites of 4-H cows, collected from estate sales over the years. The name "Mrs. Howdy" was just too adorable and a perfect accompaniment to the Howdy sign that hangs in my kitchen. But I was out of time and rushed out, thinking I'd come back soon to get my perfect little apron.

Unfortunately, when I returned it was gone. It was my "one that got away" story and I talked about it for a long time. A few days later, Teri stopped by with a package. It was my perfect little apron and she had known it the moment she saw it. And now, I love it even more.

~ Serena

Appetizers

garlic chicken pizza squares

MAKES 1 TEN-INCH PIZZA (16 APPETIZERS)
WORKING TIME 20 MINUTES
TOTAL TIME 35 MINUTES

Letting the dressing-tossed chicken rest while you prepare the other ingredients in this recipe means the flavors blend especially well. To make it more garlicky, add a bit of minced garlic to the dressing or use garlic-flavored olive oil. Cut the pizza into small slices and serve warm. Shown on page 54.

. . . .

$1^1/_2$ cups diced cooked chicken
(about $1^1/_2$ pounds)

3 tablespoons thick-style ranch dressing

Pizza dough (purchased or homemade) for 1 pizza, at room temperature

Olive oil, for drizzling

4 ounces mozzarella cheese, shredded (1 cup)

3 tablespoons sliced green onions

$1/_2$ cup diced fresh tomatoes

$1/_8$ teaspoon garlic powder

HERBED PIZZA DOUGH

You might like to enhance the flavor of your pizza dough by working in some fresh or dried herbs like garlic, rosemary, basil, or oregano. If you make your own dough, you could also exchange the plain olive oil for a flavored version. We love the Thin and Crispy Pizza Dough recipe from www.countryliving.com.

Prepare the topping: Mix the chicken and ranch dressing in a medium-size bowl until the chicken is thoroughly coated; set aside at room temperature.

Prebake the dough: Heat the oven to 400°F. Lightly oil a baking sheet. Pat the pizza dough into a 10-inch round on a lightly floured board. Transfer it to the prepared baking sheet; drizzle with olive oil. Bake until just firm—8 to 10 minutes.

Bake the pizza: Remove the baking sheet from the oven and arrange the chicken mixture, mozzarella, green onions, and tomatoes evenly over the dough. Sprinkle the garlic powder evenly over the top. Bake until the crust is brown and the cheese is melted—6 to 10 minutes longer. Cut into small squares or wedges and serve.

Nutrition per appetizer—Protein: 5.2 G; Fat: 6.4 G; Carbohydrate: 2.7 G; Fiber: 0.1 G; Sodium: 71.1 MG; Cholesterol: 17.6 MG; Calories: 89.

olivada crostini

MAKES ABOUT 1 CUP SPREAD
(ABOUT 30 APPETIZERS)
WORKING TIME 25 MINUTES
TOTAL TIME 30 MINUTES

This is one of my all-time favorites, adapted from my Aunt Erin's recipe. The blend of olives, Parmesan, and a hint of vinegar makes the flavor similar to a muffuletta sandwich spread. You can serve the topping warm, toasted on baguette slices, or at room temperature in a little dish with fresh baguette slices on the side. Whenever I serve these, someone requests the recipe. ~Serena Shown on page 54.

- 1 4.25-ounce can chopped black olives
- 1/3 cup chopped pimiento-stuffed green olives
- 1/4 cup chopped jarred roasted red bell peppers
- 3 ounces Parmesan cheese, shredded (3/4 cup)
- 2 tablespoons red wine vinegar
- 1/4 cup olive oil
- 2 cloves garlic, minced
- 1 French baguette, cut into 1/2-inch thick slices

Mix the black and green olives, peppers, Parmesan, vinegar, oil, and garlic in a small bowl until combined. If you wish to serve the crostini warm, heat the broiler, arrange the baguette slices on a large baking sheet and place about 3 inches from the heat until lightly browned—1 to 2 minutes. Remove from the broiler, add a heaping teaspoonful of the olive mixture to the browned side of each slice, and return to the broiler just until the mixture is warm and the cheese is bubbly—1 to 2 minutes more. Transfer to a serving plate and serve.

Nutrition per appetizer—Protein: 2.4 G; Fat: 3.9 G; Carbohydrate: 6.5 G; Fiber: 0.5 G; Sodium: 178.2 MG; Cholesterol: 2.5 MG; Calories: 70.

aprons from vintage sheets

We've always worn aprons at our antiques show, using the pockets to keep our supplies such as markers, tape, and papers close at hand. We started getting requests for them and decided to start making them to sell at our shows. We really love the good quality cotton in old sheets and began collecting them at yard sales and thrift shops over the next year. What we found is that old sheets are readily available and not a highly sought after item, which tends to make them really inexpensive. We collect both patterned and plain vintage sheets, which gives a lot of options for designs. Our collection of old sheets continues to grow and we hope yours will too!

Before you cut your sheets following your chosen apron pattern, launder them in hot water. If there are any stains, soak in your favorite stain remover. We prefer OxiClean. (If stains persist, simply avoid them when you lay out your pattern pieces.) When clean and dry, iron the sheets; then lay out your pattern and cut it out. If you prefer a lined apron, we recommend using a patterned vintage sheet on the front and a vintage white sheet on the back. Sew the apron according to the pattern directions.

Not only are these aprons highly functional, they're great for gift giving too. Package one with your favorite linen spray, add some recipe cards to the pocket, and you've got the perfect little gift for someone you love.

Tie on an Apron

When I get dressed in the morning, I put on an apron. It's become such a habit that if I don't, I feel undressed and unprotected. I have about five or six in the rotation. Some are coming apart at the seams, some are threadbare and all are stained from cleaning and cooking. I started wearing one because it was practical and frankly, I'm a messy cook and I've stained more than a few shirts, and now it's a habit. Serena and I like to say that the first step in any recipe should be to tie on your apron. My first apron was a Christmas gift at age five. Mom made it from scraps of material she had leftover from some project. I remember wearing that little waist apron while helping Mom in the kitchen and outside while making mud pies. Both of my girls wore it while helping me and it's folded and packed away in my basement ready for future grandchildren. So, whether you prefer a little waist apron or if you need more protection and require a full apron, tie one on and you'll be hooked.

~Teri

❄ cheese toasts

MAKES ABOUT 1 CUP TOPPING (ABOUT 30 APPETIZERS)
WORKING TIME 15 MINUTES
TOTAL TIME 25 MINUTES

This is a quick make-ahead recipe for a busy party night. You can prepare and chill the cheese spread and cut and bake the baguette slices up to two days in advance. Then all you'll need to do before the party is spread the cheese on each slice and bake for a few minutes.

- $^1/_2$ cup mayonnaise
- 2 ounces sharp Cheddar cheese, grated ($^1/_2$ cup)
- 2 cloves garlic, minced
- $^1/_4$ cup sliced green onions
- 1 baguette, cut into $^1/_2$-inch thick slices

Heat the oven to 350°F. Mix the mayonnaise, cheese, garlic, and green onions in a small bowl. Arrange the baguette slices on a baking sheet and bake until golden brown—8 to 10 minutes. Spread a couple teaspoonfuls of the cheese mixture on each slice and bake until the cheese is melted and bubbly—2 to 3 minutes more. Transfer to a serving plate and serve.

Nutrition per appetizer—Protein: 1.7 G; Fat: 3.8 G; Carbohydrate: 6 G; Fiber: 0.3 G; Sodium: 103.8 MG; Cholesterol: 3.3 MG; Calories: 65.

Tasty Dill Chips

Here's a quick, easy way to give plain potato chips a bit of an upscale taste: Spread the chips on a baking sheet and evenly sprinkle with dried dill weed. Bake for 5 minutes in a heated 350°F oven. We use a ratio of 1 teaspoon dried dill to a 4-ounce bag of kettle-style chips; you could use a different favorite herb, for instance rosemary, if you wish. Serve them as a nibble or with sandwiches, as we show in the photo on page 76.

PLACE MARKERS

1. The fabric needs to be pretty stiff in order for the markers to stand up on their own. If your fabric isn't really heavy, (like upholstery fabric) spray each piece generously with starch, or reinforce with a heavyweight fusible interfacing (from a fabric or crafts supply store).

2. With the right side out, fold each fabric piece in half, bringing the 3 1/2-inch edges together, and press the crease with an iron.

3. For the name background, choose a contrasting solid-color fabric and cut it into small rectangles with pinking shears.

4. Using rubber stamps and ink of your choosing, stamp the name for each marker onto one of the rectangles. Hand lettered names look great too.

5. Center each name-stamped rectangle on one face of a piece of folded fabric and hot-glue into place.

For a dolled-up table, we created these place markers out of a recent flea-market find: vintage textile samples and old rubber stamps. Many of the fabric samples came as small rectangles, measuring 5 by 3 1/2 inches, which were the perfect size for these. You can begin your place markers by cutting a heavy fabric of your choosing to that same size.

We have a large variety of vintage letter stamps that we've collected over the years. Almost all have been found in thrift shops in unmarked boxes at the bottom of shelves and at yard sales in the free box or trash pile. Don't be afraid to dig!

STAMP FIRST

You might find it easier to stamp the names on the solid-color fabric before cutting it into small rectangles. That way you can be sure the stamping is centered on each little piece.

LOIS AND VERN

Lois and Vern were in a tough position. Lois's childhood home, deep in the heart of the Palouse, had become a liability. It hadn't been lived in for many years and was becoming unsafe. They made the decision to burn it down, but not before they invited us to purchase its contents.

The home, which was surrounded by acres of wheat and lentils, had been in Lois's family for many generations. Lois's grandmother had been married to a traveling salesman who sold livestock remedies, beauty products, toiletries, spices, and basic household supplies to farm families in Eastern Washington and Northern Idaho in the 1920s. Her grandmother had also been a jewelry saleswoman.

Vern, Lois, and all of their family had been through the house many times taking what they wanted. The remaining contents were left in place, awaiting the local

fire department to use the burn as a training project. We were thrilled that they contacted us. We grabbed our gloves, packed a lunch, and hitched up the trailer. It took hours to go through the house, attic, barn, and chicken coop. We discovered case after case of inventory, much of it still in its original packaging, unopened and unused, lots of old household items, and farm treasures. We had so much fun, each squealing for the other to "come look what I found!"

We made several trips out to the farm and during those visits, Vern and Lois were kind enough to share the history of the farm and stories of their family. How Lois was late for their wedding because she had fallen and skinned her knee and how Vern had begun to fear that she had changed her mind. They shared stories of raising a household of girls and life on the farm. Lois showed us photos and keepsakes from a memory box, telling us the stories behind the photos. We made a copy of one and used it for one of our show reminder postcards.

On our drive home that last trip out, we relived the day, wondering how we got so lucky. Not only did we find some amazing things, we were again reminded that there are lives and memories connected to the "junk" we find. We both have items in our homes reminding us of that special adventure, of the beautiful countryside, and, of course, Vern and Lois.

tangy cucumber cups

MAKES ABOUT 24 CUCUMBER CUPS
WORKING TIME 35 MINUTES
TOTAL TIME 1 HOUR AND 5 MINUTES

It's always nice to add some vegetables into a mix of appetizers. This light, make-ahead nibble is a take on my favorite cucumber salad. Simply fill the cupped slices with the "dressing" and your crisp, cold appetizer is ready for the party tray. ~ Teri

1 large English cucumber
(about 18 to 20 inches in length)

$^1/_3$ cup rice wine vinegar

2 tablespoons honey

$^1/_4$ cup sour cream

2 tablespoons mayonnaise

$^1/_4$ cup chopped red onion

$^1/_4$ cup crumbled feta cheese (1 ounce)

$^1/_2$ teaspoon dried dill weed

$^1/_8$ teaspoon salt

THE RIGHT CUCUMBER

English cucumbers are the extra-long type that is virtually seedless. They're sometimes called "hothouse" cucumbers.

Cut the cucumber: Cut off and discard the cucumber ends. To make the cups decorative, peel off a stripe along each of three sides on the cucumber; then cut it crosswise into $^3/_4$-inch thick slices. Making sure to not go all the way through, scoop out and discard a little from the center of each slice using a $^1/_2$-teaspoon measuring spoon; set aside the slice "cups."

Marinate the cups: Whisk together the vinegar and honey in a small bowl. Add the cucumber cups; cover tightly and marinate for 30 minutes in the refrigerator.

Prepare the dressing: Meanwhile, whisk together the sour cream and mayonnaise in a medium-size bowl. Mix in the red onion, feta cheese, dill, and salt.

Assemble the cups: Remove the cucumber cups from the marinade and fill each with approximately 1 teaspoon of the dressing. Arrange on a serving plate, cover, and refrigerate until ready to serve.

Tangy Cucumber Cups shown opposite with Sour Cream & Onion Zucchini Cakes, page 66.

Nutrition per cucumber cup—Protein: 0.6 G; Fat: 1.7 G; Carbohydrate: 1.9 G; Fiber: 0.3 G; Sodium: 34.3 MG; Cholesterol: 2.5 MG; Calories: 24.

sour cream & onion zucchini cakes

MAKES ABOUT 18 TWO-INCH CAKES
WORKING TIME 45 MINUTES
TOTAL TIME 1 HOUR AND 45 MINUTES

The flavor of this yummy, small version of a zucchini fritter reminds us of our favorite sour-cream-and-onion potato chips. Be sure to give the grated zucchini a good squeeze before mixing in the remaining ingredients—you'll get the best results from removing as much liquid as possible. Forming the little cakes is a sticky process, but well worth the mess. Shown on page 65.

PANKO BREAD CRUMBS

Years ago, while visiting my sister Kathy in Seattle, I stopped by a specialty market and picked up some Japanese-style panko bread crumbs. I had never heard of them before and thought I'd give them a try. They're a bit coarser than ordinary bread crumbs and give dishes a lighter, crunchier texture. I rarely use any other type now, and luckily, most markets carry them. I keep a good supply in my pantry. ~Teri

2 cups grated zucchini (about 3 medium zucchini)

1 large egg, lightly beaten

2 tablespoons all-purpose flour, plus $1/2$ cup for coating cakes

$3/4$ cup panko bread crumbs

$1/4$ cup finely diced onion

$1/4$ teaspoon salt

$1/4$ teaspoon fresh ground black pepper

Vegetable oil, for frying

Sour cream, for serving (about $1/2$ cup)

Chopped fresh chives, for serving

Drain the zucchini: Place the grated zucchini on a paper towel–lined plate and let it sit for an hour; occasionally change the paper towel.

Mix the cakes: With your hands, transfer the zucchini to a medium-size bowl, tightly squeezing as you do so to remove as much liquid as possible. Add the egg, the 2 tablespoons flour, bread crumbs, onion, salt, and pepper; mix to combine.

Fry the cakes: Place the remaining $1/2$ cup flour on a plate. Add enough oil to a medium-size skillet to be $1/8$-inch deep; heat over medium-high heat until hot. Meanwhile, form the zucchini mixture into tiny (2-inch) bite-sized cakes. Working in three batches, pat each side of each cake in the flour and place in the hot skillet. Fry on each side until golden brown—1 to 2 minutes. Transfer to a paper towel–lined plate to drain. Arrange the cakes on a serving plate, top each with a dollop of sour cream, and sprinkle with chives. Serve warm.

Nutrition per cake with sour cream—Protein: 1.7 G; Fat: 3.6 G; Carbohydrate: 7.7 G; Fiber: 0.5 G; Sodium: 48.9 MG; Cholesterol: 14.6 MG; Calories: 67.

parmesan rice–
stuffed mushrooms

MAKES 24 MUSHROOMS
WORKING TIME 35 MINUTES
TOTAL TIME 50 MINUTES

While out with our husbands at dinner one night, we had an appetizer of portobello mushrooms topped with risotto. We decided to try to re-create it, but opted for a simpler version made with white mushrooms and rice. Cooking the rice in chicken broth adds to the flavor, so does sautéing the mushroom stems. This rice stuffing would be just as tasty in a tomato or red bell pepper.

. . . .

$1/2$ cup uncooked white rice

1 cup chicken broth

24 medium to large white mushrooms (about $1^1/4$ pounds)

2 tablespoons butter

1 teaspoon white wine

$1/2$ cup half-and-half or heavy cream

$1/2$ cup grated Parmesan cheese (2 ounces)

2 tablespoons chopped fresh parsley

Salt to taste (optional)

Cook the rice and mushrooms: Heat the oven to 350°F. Cook the rice according to the package directions, substituting the chicken broth for water. While the rice is cooking, clean the mushrooms by brushing with a clean dishcloth. Remove the stems and reserve. Place the mushroom caps smooth side up on a baking sheet. Bake for 12 minutes.

Drain the mushroom caps and cook the stems: Remove the mushroom caps from the oven (leave the oven on) and transfer them, smooth side up, to a paper towel–lined plate to drain. Meanwhile, chop the mushroom stems. Heat the butter in a medium-size skillet over medium heat; add the chopped stems and sauté for 5 to 6 minutes. Add the white wine and remove from the heat.

Stuff and bake the mushrooms: When the rice is fully cooked, stir in the sautéed mushroom stems with any juices, half-and-half, Parmesan, and parsley; if desired, add salt to taste. Turn each mushroom cap over (gills up) and fill each with approximately 1 tablespoon of the rice mixture; place on a clean baking sheet. Bake for 12 to 14 minutes. Serve warm.

Nutrition per mushroom—Protein: 1.9 G; Fat: 2.2 G; Carbohydrate: 4.4 G; Fiber: 0.3 G; Sodium: 74.2 MG; Cholesterol: 5.8 MG; Calories: 44.

WINE FOR COOKING

We have a few recipes that call for a little bit of white wine. I didn't like the idea of opening a big bottle for a recipe that called for just two tablespoons so I usually just skipped that step. Even though the specified wine quantity was small, I knew it added a lot of flavor. I was pleased to discover that my grocery market carries quite a variety of wine in miniature bottles. They come in a four-pack and are about 6 ounces each. They're the perfect size for the pantry. If wine isn't sold at your grocery, look for small bottles at a wine merchant. ~Teri

COOKBOOK JACKETS

We both collect old cookbooks, which tend to be worn from years of use. We created these quick, simple jackets to protect them. In some cases, we've found cookbooks on which the front or back cover has been torn loose and have been able to repair them using heavy tape. Add a jacket like these and the repair can't be seen. Best of all, you can use old (unused) shower curtains or inexpensive new vinyl tablecloths to make the jackets—the prints are fun and the surface is easy to wipe clean.

1. Lay your material flat, wrong side up. Place the cookbook atop the material. Open cookbook near its middle, flattening as much as possible. Cut out the material with margins of $1/2$ inch on the top and bottom of the cookbook, and 2 inches on each side.

2. Fold the 2-inch margins over the book cover on each side and temporarily secure at the top and bottom with a paper clip. Close the cookbook to make sure the jacket is big enough; loosen the material if you need to. Remove the cookbook, and paper clip the folds in the material to keep in place.

3. With a sewing machine, sew all the way across the top of the jacket about $3/8$ inch from the edge; sew across the bottom edge the same way. Trim the excess material just above the stitching. Slip the cookbook into the jacket.

CREASE REMOVAL
To remove fold lines or wrinkles from vinyl, place it in your dryer on low heat for 1 to 2 minutes. Watch carefully. Remove the vinyl and lay it flat.

sweet onion tartlets

MAKES 24 TARTLETS
WORKING TIME 45 MINUTES
TOTAL TIME 1 HOUR AND 20 MINUTES

This delicious bite-sized appetizer is the perfect treat for people who love onions—especially caramelized onions. You'll be surprised at the sweet and savory combination. We are partial to Walla Walla onions, but any sweet onion variety will do. Shown on page 70.

$3/4$ cup butter ($1^1/_2$ sticks), softened

1 3-ounce package cream cheese, at room temperature

1 cup all-purpose flour

4 cups quartered and thinly sliced sweet onions (about 3 large)

2 teaspoons sugar

$1/_2$ teaspoon salt

$1/_3$ cup heavy cream

1 large egg

Make the crust: Heat the oven to 350°F. Combine $1/_2$ cup (1 stick) butter and the cream cheese in a medium-size bowl and mix with a wooden spoon until smooth. Add the flour and mix until well combined. Scoop the mixture into 24 heaping teaspoonfuls and roll each into a ball. Press each ball into the bottom and up the sides of an ungreased mini-tart (muffin) pan; set aside.

Cook the onions: Heat a large skillet over medium high heat. Add the remaining $1/_4$ cup ($1/_2$ stick) butter, stirring until melted; then add the onions, stir in the sugar and salt, and sauté over medium-low heat until golden brown and caramelized—20 minutes. Divide the onion mixture evenly between the 24 tartlet shells.

Bake the tartlets: Combine the cream and egg in a glass measuring cup and whisk until smooth. Pour into the tartlets, dividing evenly. Bake until the filling and crust are golden brown—22 to 24 minutes. Transfer the tartlets from the baking pan to a serving plate and serve warm.

Nutrition per tartlet—Protein: 1.4 G; Fat: 8.4 G; Carbohydrate: 6.5 G; Fiber: 0.4 G; Sodium: 105.7 MG; Cholesterol: 32.2 MG; Calories: 106.

TART TAMPER
I've fallen in love with a little wooden gadget that is great for smoothing dough in tartlet pans. Once you've rolled your dough into little balls, simply press down on each piece with the tamper and it instantly spreads out the dough, pushing it evenly up the sides. ~Serena

grilled cumin chicken with apricot dipping sauce

MAKES ABOUT 24 APPETIZERS
WORKING TIME 30 MINUTES
TOTAL TIME 2 HOURS AND 35 MINUTES

The idea for this appetizer came from one of our favorite grilled chicken dinners, which we usually served topped with a peanut sauce. After learning that neither of our husbands cares for peanut sauce, we came up with this really simple jam dipping sauce as an alternative.

$^1\!/_2$ cup sour cream

1 tablespoon honey

1 teaspoon hot red-pepper sauce

1 large clove garlic, minced

$^1\!/_2$ teaspoon ground cumin

$^1\!/_4$ teaspoon salt

2 skinless, boneless chicken breast halves (about 12 ounces)

Apricot Dipping Sauce (recipe follows)

Make the marinade: Mix together the sour cream, honey, hot-pepper sauce, garlic, cumin, and salt in a medium-size bowl; set aside.

Prepare the chicken and dipping sauce: Cut the chicken breasts into large bite-size pieces (you should have approximately 2 cups). Add to the bowl with the marinade and toss to combine. Cover and refrigerate for at least 2 hours. Meanwhile, prepare the Apricot Dipping Sauce.

Grill the chicken: Heat an outdoor grill to medium high. Place a lightly greased mesh grill topper on the grill. Grill the chicken until cooked through—about 4 minutes, turning once. Remove the chicken from the grill. Insert a toothpick into each piece and arrange on a serving plate. Serve with the sauce.

Apricot Dipping Sauce

Combine $^1\!/_4$ cup apricot jam with 2 tablespoons plain yogurt in a small bowl. Cover and refrigerate if not serving shortly; allow to reach room temperature before serving.

Nutrition per appetizer with sauce—Protein: 3.1 G; Fat: 1 G; Carbohydrate: 2.9 G; Fiber: 0 G; Sodium: 27.7 MG; Cholesterol: 9 MG; Calories: 33.

Grilled Cumin Chicken with Apricot Dipping Sauce shown opposite with Sweet Onion Tarlets, page 69.

CHALKBOARDS & ERASERS

Please leave your boots at the door

Ethan's Chores...
Make Bed
feed dog
weed garden

Who doesn't love a chalkboard? They've become popular in both the country and modern home. Use them to keep track of needed groceries, schedules, or weekly menus. We both have one by our front door where everyone from friends to delivery services can leave messages. Add a fabric or wallpaper-embellished eraser to make updating the messages more fun.

With special paint, you can transform any object with a flat, smooth surface into a blackboard. We've used a drawer, dustpan, enamelware baking pan (see page 6), and an old kitchen cupboard door. Chalkboard paint comes in both liquid and spray versions and you can find it in crafts, art supply, and paint stores.

1. Prep the surface of your chosen flat object by lightly sanding it to help the chalkboard paint go on smoothly. Mask the edges of the chalkboard area with blue painter's tape to ensure the paint goes only where you want it to. If you're using spray paint, be sure to cover the surrounding area carefully to prevent spatter.

2. Apply two coats of chalkboard paint, letting dry between coats as indicated on the can. If you're using liquid paint, apply it with a small sponge applicator or roller, as the fibers in regular paintbrushes tend to leave streaks.

3. To give a standard eraser retro appeal, cut a scrap of fabric or printed paper to the size of the back and then glue it in place with white glue. To convert a wooden block to an eraser, cut a piece of felt to the size of one surface and glue it in place with white glue.

brown sugar bacon bites

MAKES 24 APPETIZERS
WORKING TIME 20 MINUTES
TOTAL TIME 1 HOUR

Some of the best recipes are those that are the easiest. The hint of sweetness and crunchy texture make these nibbles unusually delicious. If the water chestnuts are too big for the bacon pieces, simply cut them in half.

- -

8 thick slices bacon, cut crosswise into thirds

1 5-ounce can whole peeled water chestnuts, drained

1/3 cup brown sugar

Heat the oven to 375°F. Line a baking sheet with foil. Wrap each piece of bacon around a water chestnut; secure with a toothpick and place seam-side down on the baking sheet. Sprinkle the tops with the brown sugar. Bake until the bacon begins to crisp—35 to 40 minutes. Arrange on a serving plate and serve warm.

Nutrition per appetizer—Protein: 1.4 G; Fat: 1.7 G; Carbohydrate: 3.5 G; Fiber: 0.2 G; Sodium: 84.7 MG; Cholesterol: 3.3 MG; Calories: 34.

TINY THINGS

What is it about miniature items that we're drawn to? It doesn't matter what it is, if it's tiny, it's so darn cute! Maybe because they're child-sized, they seem more precious. We love serving coffee cream and maple syrup in tiny little creamers, using old, silver baby spoons for serving jam and dips, and serving up appetizers with itty-bitty tongs. And of course, butter pats always make a meal feel extra special. Maybe that's why most of us choose to celebrate festive occasions with appetizers. That perfect combination of tiny and yummy just seems to make us happy!

mad for vintage cookbooks

*B*e they new or old, we love cookbooks. We've both bought vintage cookbooks just because we thought the cover was adorable and if we find a good recipe inside, it's a bonus! We also enjoy the whimsical and colorful illustrations found in many of these books.

Old cookbooks remind us of a simpler time when families were less mobile and shared meals together on a regular basis. Running out for dinner or having it delivered to the door wasn't an option, so meals were carefully planned. The thoughtful tips found in wartime and Depression-era cookbooks are practical, economical, and still hold true today. We especially enjoy the occasional story and love reading about the history of a recipe, so many of which were handed down from earlier generations or created out of necessity. Reading vintage cookbooks offers a connection to the past and is almost like reading a history book!

As much as we both love old cookbooks, we enjoy them more for their inspiration than their usefulness. The language and terms used in older cookbooks tend to be different from what we're used to now. The way things were measured isn't always as we do today and temperature settings and baking times have altered quite a bit as a lot of cooks once used wood-burning stoves. Although we greatly admire the cooks from other eras, we're grateful for the kitchen conveniences of today. But we've had pretty good luck recreating old baking recipes, finding that most can be quite easily adapted for modern equipment and techniques.

For us, the tricky part of our passion for vintage cookbooks is finding a place to keep them conveniently located and displayed. Count yourself lucky if you have built-in bookshelves in your kitchen for your cookbooks, but even if you don't, there are many ways to creatively display them. If you like to collect old things you may have something right now in your home that you can use such as:

★ Vintage metal picnic baskets
★ Old locker baskets
★ Metal milk crates
★ Old colorful dish drainers
★ Vintage pedestal cake plates

If you already have your cookbooks on a shelf, on top of your refrigerator or even lined up on your counter, you can dress them up by using fun bookends such as these vintage items (fill lightweight containers with dried rice or beans):

★ Colorful thermoses
★ Coffee tins
★ Canning jars with colorful candies
★ Funky old canisters
★ Great old kitchen scales
★ Milk bottles with graphic labels

Start your own little collection of vintage cookbooks. Even if you don't use them for recipe ideas, you'll be inspired by the hardworking, creative, and ever-resourceful women of past generations.

✳ *Lunch* ✳

toasted turkey melt

MAKES 4 SERVINGS
WORKING TIME 10 MINUTES
TOTAL TIME 15 MINUTES

The inspiration for this sandwich came from a favorite hangout of ours that has since closed. We just had to re-create it. It's warm and toasty and full of flavor. Shown on page 76.

- -

6 tablespoons finely chopped jarred
roasted red bell peppers

4 teaspoons liquid from roasted pepper jar

½ cup mayonnaise

4 large slices country sourdough bread,
½-inch thick

4 thin slices havarti cheese

6 thin slices roasted deli turkey

Thinly sliced red onion (optional)

Prepare the sandwiches: Mix the peppers, pepper liquid, and mayonnaise in a small bowl. Spread the mixture onto each bread slice, dividing equally. Make 2 large sandwiches, layering 3 slices of turkey, 2 slices of cheese, and some onion, if using, on each of 2 bread slices; top each with another bread slice.

Cook the sandwiches: Lightly oil a large skillet with vegetable oil or cooking spray and heat it over medium heat. Add the sandwiches and cook until the cheese is melted and bread is toasty, turning once—about 1 minute per side. Cut each big sandwich in half to make 4 servings and serve warm.

Nutrition per serving—Protein: 22 G; Fat: 33.1 G; Carbohydrate: 34.1 G; Fiber: 1.6 G; Sodium: 1181.5 MG; Cholesterol: 50 MG; Calories: 527.

roasted chicken & pesto hoagies

MAKES 4 SANDWICHES
WORKING TIME 10 MINUTES
TOTAL TIME 15 MINUTES

This is such a delicious and easy-to-fix sandwich—the pesto and warm melted cheese make it unforgettable. We like it made with the breast meat from a rotisserie chicken from our local market; you can roast your own if you prefer. Just tear the meat with into bite-size pieces with your fingers. Shown on page 76.

4 hoagie rolls (hero rolls)

½ cup basil pesto

2 cups shredded rotisserie chicken breast meat

8 thin slices provolone cheese

Heat the broiler. Separate the rolls and arrange the halves on a baking sheet. Spread pesto on each half, dividing equally. Divide the chicken among 4 of the halves; top with 2 slices of the cheese. Place under the broiler, 4 to 6 inches from the heat source, until the cheese is melted—1 to 2 minutes. Put the 2 halves of each sandwich together and serve warm.

Nutrition per sandwich—Protein: 49.7 G; Fat: 37.8 G; Carbohydrate: 36.9 G; Fiber: 3 G; Sodium: 1047.6 MG; Cholesterol: 124.4 MG; Calories: 689.

veggie pitas

MAKES 4 SANDWICHES
WORKING TIME 15 MINUTES
TOTAL TIME 15 MINUTES

Nothing beats this cool, crisp veggie pita on a hot summer day. This filling combination is our favorite, but other vegetables such as green peppers, black olives, or shredded carrots would be very tasty too.

8 ounces cream cheese, softened

2 green onions, chopped (1/4 cup)

2 large pocket-style pitas, halved

1 ripe large tomato, sliced

1 ripe medium avocado, sliced

1/2 English cucumber, sliced into thin rounds

2 cups alfalfa sprouts

Olive oil and red wine vinegar
for drizzling

Mix the cream cheese and green onions in a small bowl until combined. Spread the mixture inside each pita half, dividing equally. Layer in the tomato, avocado, and cucumber. Divide the alfalfa sprouts among the pockets and then drizzle oil and vinegar into each pocket.

Nutrition per sandwich without oil and vinegar—Protein: 9.1 G; Fat: 25.6 G; Carbohydrate: 24.3 G; Fiber: 4.2 G; Sodium: 334.6 MG; Cholesterol: 62.4 MG; Calories: 354.

COUNTERTOP UTENSIL HOLDER

I don't have many options for conveniently storing kitchen utensils. The two tiny drawers on either side of my stove don't offer a good solution. So I've used everything from a pitcher to an old coffee tin, but we really like the idea of this simple glass jar dressed up with colorful oilcloth (for more about oilcloth, see page 119). Best of all, the liner can be easily changed to suit the colors of the season or my mood. ~Teri

1. Find a new or vintage glass jar that is large enough to hold the amount of utensils to be kept at hand. Thoroughly wash the jar—inside and out. Allow to dry completely.

2. Wrap a tape measure around the jar to see how long the liner needs to be, and also measure the height of the smooth section of the jar side. Cut a piece of oilcloth to these dimensions.

3. Insert the oilcloth in the jar, making sure the patterned face is toward the glass. The surface of oilcloth has a bit of a grip to it, making it perfect for this project as it clings to the side of the glass. If necessary, adhere the overlapping edges together with a few dabs of hot glue.

VINYL WORKS TOO

A vinyl tablecloth will work too, but the surface is slippery and won't stay upright by itself. To keep it in place, glue the overlapping ends together or sew the vinyl lining into a tube before inserting it in the jar.

'mater sandwiches

MAKES 4 SANDWICHES
WORKING TIME 20 MINUTES
TOTAL TIME 20 MINUTES

At the mill where my husband works, they have a "'Mater Sandwich Day" during tomato season. We've updated the basic tomatoes, white bread, and mayo version with a cheesy garlic spread, inspired by our favorite local Junior League dip recipe. ~Teri

½ cup sour cream	1 teaspoon fresh lemon juice
¼ cup crumbled feta cheese (1 ounce)	¼ teaspoon dried dill weed
¼ cup grated Parmesan cheese (1 ounce)	⅛ teaspoon salt
2 tablespoons sliced green onions	8 ½-inch thick slices crusty bread
1 to 2 garlic cloves, minced	12 thick slices ripe tomato (about 4 medium)

Mix the sour cream, cheeses, green onions, garlic, lemon juice, dill, and salt together in a medium-size bowl until combined. Spread about 3 tablespoons dressing onto each of 4 bread slices; top with tomato slices. Cover with another slice of bread and serve.

Nutrition per sandwich—Protein: 11.2 G; Fat: 12.1 G; Carbohydrate: 41.1 G; Fiber: 2.9 G; Sodium: 687.3 MG; Cholesterol: 25.4 MG; Calories: 317.

elaine's farm style chicken salad sandwiches

MAKES 4 SANDWICHES
WORKING TIME 20 MINUTES
TOTAL TIME 20 MINUTES

These sandwiches evoke special memories for us. Our dear friend Elaine made them for us at our first antiques show in another friend's barn. Elaine's secret is roasting the chicken with her favorite spices to give it great flavor. The salad is great served on greens if you don't want sandwiches.

2 boneless skinless chicken breast halves (1¼ pounds)

½ teaspoon garlic powder

1 teaspoon dried basil

½ teaspoon dried rosemary

½ teaspoon salt

½ teaspoon ground black pepper

¾ cup mayonnaise

⅓ cup finely chopped celery

¼ cup sliced green onions

8 ½-inch thick slices crusty bread

Cook the chicken: Heat the oven to 350°F. Place the chicken breasts in a shallow baking dish with 1 cup of water. Sprinkle with the garlic powder, basil, rosemary, ¼ teaspoon salt, and ¼ teaspoon pepper. Cover with aluminum foil and bake until cooked through—25 to 30 minutes. Remove the chicken from the baking dish to a plate. When cool enough to handle, cut the chicken into bite-size pieces (you should have about 2 cups).

Make the sandwiches: Mix the mayonnaise, celery, green onions, and remaining ¼ teaspoon salt and pepper in a medium-size bowl. Add the chicken and stir to coat. Divide equally atop 4 of the bread slices; top with the remaining 4 slices.

Nutrition per sandwich—Protein: 35 G; Fat: 38.8 G; Carbohydrate: 36.7 G; Fiber: 2.3 G; Sodium: 1049.8 MG; Cholesterol: 93.3 MG; Calories: 650.

WAX PAPER WRAPPING

We'll never forget the way Elaine presented these sandwiches to all of us at our first antiques show. Each sandwich was beautifully wrapped in wax paper and sliced in half through the paper. They were all stacked on a huge platter and looked just as pretty as they were tasty. We were inspired by her old-fashioned presentation, and have enjoyed rediscovering the great wrapping wax paper makes.

CHERYL

We first met Cheryl when she began attending our antiques shows. When she found out that we were participating in an event in Idaho, she came to visit and shop with her sister, Jeni. When they walked into our booth, Cheryl's mouth dropped open at the sight of an old Valley Answering Service sign we had for sale.

The sign had been a last minute addition to our booth, added in by Serena, out of her home. Serena loved the sign, which we had found at a sale earlier that summer near Valley, Washington. It was in amazing condition with the darling image of a woman on the phone. Unfortunately, she was never able to find the right place to hang it in her house. After moving it several times, she realized it wasn't perfect for her home and added it into our truckload headed to Idaho.

Cheryl explained that her mom, Joan, had been a telephone operator in Valley, Washington, for many years, and that they had recently lost her to cancer. She just couldn't imagine that this was the actual sign from where her mom worked! The business had closed down many years ago. We'll never forget the look on her face when we told her that we had purchased it right near that same area. Cheryl and Jeni could hardly believe their ears.

After Cheryl got home, she hung the sign in her living room. When her father came to visit later that day, he authenticated it, remembering the sign as one that had hung outside the answering service and explained that the image of the woman on the sign was the owner's daughter.

We've had the chance to visit with Cheryl several times since then and enjoyed hearing the stories of Joan and her days as a telephone operator. This is our favorite: Joan was a city girl and not familiar with the workings of a farm, which made it tricky when fielding calls from farmers. When a farmer's animals went into heat, they'd call the operator to get through to a veterinarian. One day, a farmer called for just that reason, using the standard phrase, "My cows have come in," and Joan said, "From where?" The farmer stammered and then put his wife on the phone to explain the birds and the bees of farm animals.

We love that Cheryl now has this remembrance of her mom and get goose bumps every time we tell the story. It was only a fluke that we found the sign in the first place: We were about to call it quits for the day and decided we could make one last stop, at which point we found the sale where Serena discovered the sign. And although she couldn't quite figure out why, after a few weeks in her home, she decided the sign wasn't for her. Turns out, Serena was right, it wasn't for her. It was for Cheryl and that's the way it was meant to be.

cheesy potato soup

This soup is my daughter Allie's favorite. She always requests it when she comes home to visit from college. I like to use sharp Cheddar cheese as it has a nice strong flavor. The surprising addition of dried basil adds just the right touch. Once you try this, it'll be your favorite too. ~Teri

. . . .

4 tablespoons butter (½ stick)

1 cup diced carrots (¼-inch dice)

4 cups chicken broth (1 32-ounce carton)

5 cups peeled and cubed russet potatoes (about 4 medium; ½-inch cube)

1 teaspoon dried basil

¼ teaspoon salt

⅛ teaspoon ground black pepper

¼ cup all-purpose flour

1½ cups milk (lowfat or whole)

8 ounces sharp Cheddar cheese, grated (2 cups)

Make the soup: Melt 1 tablespoon of the butter in a large stockpot over medium-high heat. Add the carrots and sauté until softened—3 to 4 minutes. Add the broth, potatoes, basil, salt, and pepper. Bring to a boil; lower the heat and simmer until the potatoes are tender—about 20 minutes.

Make the cheese sauce: Meanwhile, melt the remaining 3 tablespoons butter in a medium-size saucepan over medium-high heat. Stir in the flour and cook for 1 minute. Slowly whisk in the milk and cook until slightly thickened—2 minutes. Add the cheese and stir until melted and thoroughly combined. Gradually pour the sauce into the soup and stir until thoroughly blended. Serve.

Nutrition per serving with whole milk—Protein: 15.1 G; Fat: 22.9 G; Carbohydrate: 35.4 G; Fiber: 3.2 G; Sodium: 1050.4 MG; Cholesterol: 65.7 MG; Calories: 405.

GO FOR SHARP

Years ago, a good friend gave me a tip that I use to this day. She suggested using only sharp Cheddar cheese in recipes. Since it has a stronger, more pungent, flavor than milder Cheddars, it's not necessary to use quite as much. Not only does it save money, but since a little goes a long way, I don't have to do as much of my least favorite kitchen chore: grating. ~Teri

savory sweet potato soup

MAKES 6 GENEROUS SERVINGS
WORKING TIME 15 MINUTES
TOTAL TIME 35 MINUTES

The combination of sweet potatoes and savory spices give this soup a really unexpected flavor. We love making this on a rainy day. For a more colorful soup, use yams instead of sweet potatoes.

4 tablespoons butter (1/2 stick)

2 cups finely chopped onions
(3 to 4 medium)

6 cups chicken broth

5 cups peeled and cubed fresh sweet potatoes or yams (about 1 1/2 pounds)

5 cups peeled and cubed russet potatoes (about 1 1/2 pounds)

1 cup peeled and shredded russet potatoes (1 medium)

1/2 cup heavy cream

2 teaspoons ground cumin

1 teaspoon dried parsley

1/4 teaspoon salt

1/8 teaspoon ground black pepper

Melt the butter in a large stockpot over medium-high heat. Stir in the onions and sauté until softened—about 5 minutes. Add the broth and sweet potatoes. Bring to a boil, lower the heat and simmer for 10 minutes. Add the potatoes, return the soup to simmering and cook until the potatoes are soft—approximately 10 more minutes. Stir in the cream, cumin, parsley, salt, and pepper. Cook over low heat, stirring often, until heated through. Serve.

Nutrition per serving—Protein: 6.6 G; Fat: 16.3 G; Carbohydrate: 59.4 G; Fiber: 7.3 G; Sodium: 1160.6 MG; Cholesterol: 47.2 MG; Calories: 404.

CHOOSE CHUNKY OR SMOOTH

I love this soup just as the recipe is written and as we've photographed it—with chunks of soft potatoes. Teri prefers it pureed until nearly smooth. If you would like to prepare it that way, you can use an immersion blender to puree it right in the pot. ~Serena

CAMP TRAY

Camping Memories

I have a special fondness for anything "campy". Maybe it's because I live in the woods or it's a look that reminds me of all the fun camping trips I've been on. As a child, in the summer we'd pack up the tent and head to a lake somewhere in the mountains. And my husband and I raised our daughters with the same tent-camping summer vacations. I guess that's why I'm drawn to old forest service or campground signs. I've collected quite a few over the years and this little tray is as functional as it is cute. Whatever style you like, you can find ways to bring it into your house to either display, or in this case, serve up s'more fixings around the campfire.

~Teri

One summer, we found a few darling old trail markers and loved their "campy" feel. We decided they'd make adorable trays for use in our homes. We dug through our collection of old handles and quickly transformed the signs into small trays. To make your own, search for any thick old wooden sign that fits your style. Then choose sturdy handles—new or old, either will do—and screws for affixing them to the sign.

1. Thoroughly clean the wood sign with a scrub brush and warm sudsy water.

2. Let dry. Sand any rough spots if necessary.

3. Place the handles on the sign, marking the holes for the screws with a pencil. Remove the handles and drill starter holes for the screws.

4. Reposition the handles and screw them on.

creamy turkey & wild rice soup

MAKES 6 GENEROUS SERVINGS
WORKING TIME 20 MINUTES
TOTAL TIME 50 MINUTES

Don't wait for Thanksgiving leftovers to make this amazing creamy soup. You can begin with freshly roasted turkey from the deli, but if you roast a small turkey breast, you'll have just the right amount for this recipe, plus enough left over for a sandwich or two.

5 tablespoons butter

1/3 cup diced celery (1/4-inch dice)

1/2 cup diced carrots (1/4-inch dice)

1 small onion, finely chopped (about 1/2 cup)

4 cups chicken broth (1 32-ounce carton)

1 cup water

3/4 cup wild rice

2 cups diced cooked turkey (about 1 pound)

6 tablespoons all-purpose flour

1/4 teaspoon poultry seasoning

1 1/4 cups half-and-half

2 tablespoons white wine (optional)

3 slices bacon, cooked and crumbled

1/4 teaspoon salt

1/8 teaspoon ground black pepper

Make the soup: Melt 1 tablespoon of the butter in a large stockpot over medium-high heat. Add the celery, carrots, and onion, sautéing until softened—about 5 minutes. Stir in the chicken broth, water, wild rice, and turkey. Bring to a boil; then lower the heat, cover, and simmer for about 40 minutes, stirring occasionally.

Make the cream sauce: Meanwhile, melt the remaining 4 tablespoons butter in a saucepan over medium heat. Mix the flour and poultry seasoning together in a small bowl and then add to the butter; cook for 1 minute, stirring constantly. Stir in the half-and-half and cook until slightly thickened—about 1 minute. Stir the sauce into the soup. Stir in the white wine, bacon, salt, and pepper. Serve.

Nutrition per serving—Protein: 30 G; Fat: 19.6 G; Carbohydrate: 27.6 G; Fiber: 2.3 G; Sodium: 943.3 MG; Cholesterol: 121.2 MG; Calories: 409.

tortellini & italian sausage soup

MAKES 8 GENEROUS SERVINGS
WORKING TIME 30 MINUTES
TOTAL TIME 1 HOUR

This is my husband, Steve's, favorite soup. I usually make it with hot Italian sausages, but to make it a little more kid-friendly, the mild is yummy too! ~Teri

- 5 mild Italian sausages (about 1 pound)
- 2 tablespoons olive oil
- 1 medium onion, finely chopped (about 1½ cups)
- 3 cloves garlic, minced
- 2 tablespoons dried Italian seasoning

- 6 cups chicken broth
- 3 14.5-ounce cans Italian-style diced tomatoes, pureed in a blender
- 1 20-ounce bag frozen cheese tortellini

Grated Parmesan cheese for serving

Cook the sausages: Heat the sausages and 1 cup of water in a large covered skillet over medium-high heat; lower the heat to medium and steam until the sausages are cooked through—10 to 12 minutes. Transfer the sausages to a plate; discard any water remaining in the skillet. When they are cool enough to handle, cut the sausages into bite-size pieces. Heat the skillet over medium heat, add the sausage pieces, and cook, stirring occasionally, until browned—3 to 4 minutes. Transfer the sausage to a paper towel–lined plate to drain.

Make the soup: Heat the olive oil in a large stockpot over medium-high heat. Add the onion and sauté until softened—3 to 4 minutes. Stir in the garlic and Italian seasoning; cook 1 minute. Stir in the broth and tomatoes; bring to simmering. Stir in the sausage and tortellini; cook until the tortellini is tender— 10 to 12 minutes. Serve, passing the Parmesan at the table.

Nutrition per serving without cheese—Protein: 17.7 G; Fat: 17.3 G; Carbohydrate: 51.1 G; Fiber: 3.4 G; Sodium: 1885.9 MG; Cholesterol: 46.3 MG; Calories: 432.

countertop
spice holders

When baking or cooking, it's nice to have spices close at hand. It is even nicer if they are sitting pretty in an adorable container! We bought this sweet little child's toy refrigerator at a local antiques shop to use in a display at the Country Living Fair. It now holds baking supplies in Teri's kitchen, while Serena keeps her spices in a tin toy barn. A dollhouse or miniature cabin would be just as cute. Millions of children played with toys like these and they're not too hard to find. Watch for them at your local antiques shop or online auction sites. Whatever you choose, it'll be sure to "spice" up your kitchen!

We suggest choosing a metal toy for a spice holder because it will clean up easily. Bring one of your spice tins and a measuring tape with you to the antiques store to make sure the toy is the size you want and need. If the bottom of the toy is rough, affix small felt bumpers (found at the hardware store) to it to protect your countertop.

If transferring spices and herbs into cute little labeled jars or tins, be sure to make a note of each expiration date.

SPICE STORAGE TIPS

Little ingredients that add big flavor, spices and herbs make a dish come alive. While creating our Cardamom Griddlecakes (page 42), we learned that spices don't last forever: We had to keep adding more and more cardamom in order to get the amount of flavor we wanted. When we reached 3 teaspoons, we realized that maybe the spice had lost its strength because it was old. We bought a new jar and remade the cakes with just a teaspoon! Freshness makes a huge difference.

Keep spices and herbs in tightly capped containers and always store away from heat. If the color and scent has faded, it's probably time to replace.

SHELF LIFE

Ground spices	
Whole spices	
Seasoning blends	*6 months*
Herbs	
Extracts	*4 years (pure vanilla lasts indefinitely)*

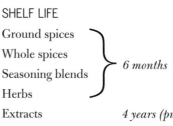

enchilada soup

We tend to have a lot of meetings over lunch and fell in love with a soup very similar to this at a local coffee shop. This is our re-creation of the delicious soup we've enjoyed so many times.

. . . .

2 tablespoons olive oil

1 medium onion, chopped (about 1 cup)

3 cloves garlic, minced

4 cups chicken broth (1 32-ounce carton)

3 cups shredded and chopped cooked chicken (about 1½ pounds)

1 15-ounce can black beans, rinsed and drained

1 14.5-ounce can petite diced tomatoes

1½ cups frozen corn kernels (about 9 ounces)

1 7-ounce can salsa verde (green salsa), or 4-ounce can chopped green chili peppers

1 tablespoon seeded and minced jalapeño pepper (1 pepper)

1 tablespoon chili powder

¼ cup cornstarch

¼ cup cold water

½ cup sour cream

Juice from half a lime

¼ cup chopped fresh cilantro

Prepare the soup: Heat the oil in a large stockpot over medium-high heat. Stir in the onion and garlic; sauté until softened—about 5 minutes. Stir in the broth, chicken, black beans, tomatoes, corn, salsa, jalapeño, and chili powder; heat to simmering.

Thicken the soup: Add the cornstarch to a small bowl; stir in the water until the mixture is smooth. Stir into the soup and simmer for 10 minutes. Whisk the sour cream and approximately 1 cup of the hot soup together in another small bowl (this step is important or the sour cream will break) until smooth; stir into the soup until well blended. Stir the lime juice and cilantro into the soup and serve.

Nutrition per serving—Protein: 36.2 G; Fat: 17.6 G; Carbohydrate: 34.9 G; Fiber: 7.4 G; Sodium: 1089 MG; Cholesterol: 93.5 MG; Calories: 446.

asian quinoa salad

MAKES 6 SIDE SERVINGS
WORKING TIME 15 MINUTES
TOTAL TIME 1 HOUR

The quinoa in this salad makes it rather delicate—we classify this as a girly salad. If quinoa isn't your style, you can always substitute orzo. If you do that, we recommend doubling the amount of dressing. No matter which you choose, you'll love the flavor.

1 small piece fresh ginger
(about 1¼ inches)

4 cups chicken broth (1 32-ounce carton)

2 cups quinoa

¼ cup plus 2 tablespoons vegetable oil

2 tablespoons rice wine vinegar

4 teaspoons peanut butter

2 teaspoons soy sauce

2 teaspoons honey

1 teaspoon sesame oil

1 to 2 cloves garlic, minced

⅓ cup diced red bell pepper
(¼-inch dice)

⅓ cup diced yellow bell pepper
(¼-inch dice)

⅓ cup sliced green onions

Roasted unsalted peanuts,
chopped, for serving (optional)

Cook the quinoa: Peel the ginger and grate enough to equal 1 teaspoon; cover and set aside. Then place the whole piece ginger in a medium-size saucepan. Add the broth and quinoa, and cook according to the quinoa package directions. Discard the ginger and transfer the quinoa to a medium-size salad bowl; set aside to cool.

Make the dressing and salad: Meanwhile, whisk together the vegetable oil, vinegar, peanut butter, soy sauce, honey, sesame oil, garlic, and reserved grated ginger in a small bowl until combined. Add the peppers and green onions to the quinoa in the salad bowl; pour the dressing over the top and toss to thoroughly combine. If you wish, sprinkle some peanuts over the salad just before serving.

Nutrition per serving without peanuts—Protein: 9.9 G; Fat: 20.4 G; Carbohydrate: 41.3 G; Fiber: 4.5 G; Sodium: 740.4 MG; Cholesterol: 0 MG; Calories: 384.

PREP AHEAD
If you wish, you can cover this salad and refrigerate up to 3 days.

FOOD COVERS

We created these pretty food covers as a way to keep picnic foods covered, in a non-plastic-wrap way. We remembered the shower cap–looking food covers that were common in the 1970s and decided that we could update them to fit our style. A bonus is that if these covers get dirty, they're washable. Choose any lightweight cotton or cotton-blend fabric you like for this project.

1. Spread the fabric wrong side up on your worktable. Invert your bowl on the fabric.

2. Measure out from rim $1\frac{1}{2}$ inches and mark a circle all the way around the bowl. Remove the bowl and cut out the fabric circle.

3. If you wish, bind the edge of the circle with bias tape. Then place the circle wrong side up in your sewing machine, with the edge under the presser foot. Lay a narrow piece of elastic on top of the edge and sew a few zigzag stitches over it. Stretch the elastic and continue to zigzag it to the edge, adjusting the elastic and your hands as needed until you've sewn all the way around.

Potluck Charm
· · · · · · · · · · · · · ·

These food covers remind me so much of the potlucks that my parents and their friends would throw throughout the summer. Potlucks were the norm in their circle and were such a great idea because it meant no food preparation stress for the host. There was always an enormous spread of food, much like a buffet, with no theme whatsoever. My sister, brother, and I always looked forward to the different types of dishes everyone would bring and many of the families had specialties they were known for. Kathy made the most amazing bean and cheese burritos, Carol's pineapple upside-down cake had the gooiest, chewiest buttery topping, and my mom and dad's barbecued chicken was deliciously sweet, spicy, and tangy.

Now that I'm a mom, summers for my family are full of camping trips, visits to our friends' lake cabins, and triathlons. I love it when our friends ask me to bring a salad or I am able to pack a picnic to enjoy after watching my husband's and children's races. Not only are my covered bowls practical, they're really cute as well.

~ Serena

 # pesto pasta salad

MAKES 4 MAIN DISH SERVINGS
WORKING TIME 15 MINUTES
TOTAL TIME 30 MINUTES

I threw this salad together for a last-minute party with friends, using what I had in my fridge. The salad was a hit and continues to be a favorite of our family and friends. ~Serena

3 cups bowtie pasta (about 8 ounces)

¼ cup basil pesto

¼ cup sour cream

1 cup chopped fresh tomatoes (about 2 medium)

½ cup halved pitted black olives

⅓ cup grated Parmesan cheese (about 1½ ounces)

¼ cup pine nuts (about 1½ ounces)

Prepare the pasta: Cook the pasta in a large pot of lightly salted boiling water according to the package directions. Drain, rinse under cold running water, drain well, and let cool. Place in a large salad bowl.

Make the salad: Mix the pesto and sour cream together in a small bowl and add to the pasta, tossing to coat. Add the tomatoes, olives, Parmesan, and pine nuts; toss to mix. Serve.

Nutrition per serving—Protein: 13.8 G; Fat: 20.5 G; Carbohydrate: 48.7 G; Fiber: 3.7 G; Sodium: 468.5 MG; Cholesterol: 17.3 MG; Calories: 429.

crunchy fiesta salad

MAKES 4 MAIN DISH SERVINGS
WORKING TIME 15 MINUTES
TOTAL TIME 30 MINUTES

Don't be hesitant about trying this surprising combination of cabbage and Southwestern flavors. It's crunchy and flavorful and holds up well, making it a perfect summertime salad. Fresh (not bottled) pico de gallo is a must for this; you can usually find it in the deli case at your market, or easily make your own (see method at right).

1½ cups fresh pico de gallo

1 cup plain yogurt

2 boneless skinless chicken breast halves (12 ounces)

½ medium head of green cabbage, cored and shredded (about 8 cups)

8 ounces sharp Cheddar cheese, grated (2 cups)

¾ cup sliced green onions

½ cup chopped cilantro

Tortilla chips (optional)

Prepare the chicken: Heat a grill to medium-high. Mix the pico de gallo and yogurt in a large bowl. Grill the chicken until cooked through, turning once—3 to 4 minutes per side. Cut into bite size pieces (you should have about 2 cups) and while still warm, add to the bowl with the pico de gallo dressing and mix together.

Make the salad: Mix the cabbage, Cheddar cheese, green onions, and cilantro in another large bowl. Add the chicken mixture and toss to coat all ingredients. If you like, crumble some tortilla chips and mix them into the salad just before serving, or pass whole chips on the side.

Nutrition per serving without chips—Protein: 36.3 G; Fat: 21.8 G; Carbohydrate: 17 G; Fiber: 3.6 G; Sodium: 868.8 MG; Cholesterol: 110 MG; Calories: 427.

FRESH PICO DE GALLO

If you'd like to make your own pico de gallo, mix equal amounts of chopped tomatoes and onions; add enough finely diced jalapeño pepper to give the heat you like. Add some chopped cilantro, minced garlic, a squeeze of lime juice, and a dash of salt to enhance the flavor. This makes a great fresh salsa for tacos, topping for tortilla soup, or salad dressing.

spinach, feta & beet salad

MAKES 6 SIDE SERVINGS
WORKING TIME 15 MINUTES
TOTAL TIME 25 MINUTES

From the sweet honey-toasted nuts to the tangy dressing—we love the combination of flavors in this pretty side salad.

³/₄ cup walnut pieces (about 5 ounces)

1 tablespoon honey

1 9-ounce package fresh spinach (approximately 12 cups)

½ cup thinly sliced red onions (1 medium)

2 tablespoons balsamic vinegar

1 teaspoon Dijon mustard

½ teaspoon salt

¼ teaspoon sugar

¼ cup olive oil

1 15-ounce can beets, rinsed, drained, and cut into bite-size pieces

½ cup crumbled feta cheese (2 ounces)

Toast the nuts: Place the walnuts in a skillet over medium heat and stir until lightly toasted—5 to 6 minutes. Add the honey and stir to coat evenly. Cook for 1 to 2 more minutes, until thoroughly coated. Transfer the mixture to a plate to cool; then break the nuts apart.

Make the salad and dressing: Place the spinach and onions in a large bowl. Whisk together the balsamic vinegar, mustard, salt, and sugar in a small bowl. Slowly whisk in the oil until thoroughly combined. Pour the dressing over the spinach and toss to coat. Divide the spinach among individual serving plates, and top each with the beets, feta, and walnuts.

Nutrition per serving—Protein: 5.8 G; Fat: 21.4 G; Carbohydrate: 12.5 G; Fiber: 2.9 G; Sodium: 480.8 MG; Cholesterol: 11.1 MG; Calories: 253.

TOASTED NUTS

Any recipe that calls for nuts will be enhanced if you toast them before adding. It's quick to do and not only brings out more flavor in the nuts, but adds to the texture as well. It just takes a quick 5 to 10 minutes in a 400°F oven or stirred in a skillet.

SHELF EDGING

Years ago, there were women just like us who, in an effort to perk up the kitchen, would put decorative edging along the shelves. The edging may have been as elaborate as hand crocheted lace or as simple as newspaper that was cut with pinking shears into decorative borders. No matter what she did, when done, each of these women surely must have stepped back and smiled to see the lift her simple little project gave her kitchen. We feel the same. A lot of homes have open shelving or glass front cupboards. What better way to perk up your kitchen? Pick up some new or vintage ribbon and trimmings and before you know it, you'll step back and smile too!

1. Cut the ribbon or other trimming to fit the length of the shelf.

2. If you wish to layer two or more trims on one shelf edge, attach them together with fabric glue or a hot glue gun. Allow to dry.

3. Separate some Velcro Sticky Back (self-adhesive) square fasteners and affix the soft halves to the shelf edge, placing one at each end and at 12-inch intervals in between. Affix the prickly halves in corresponding positions on the wrong side of your trim.

4. Position the trim over the shelf edge, lining up the Velcro squares and pressing them together.

bruschetta salad

MAKES 6 MAIN DISH SERVINGS
WORKING TIME 15 MINUTES
TOTAL TIME 25 MINUTES

This salad is a bread lover's dream. The dressing perfectly coats the ingredients and soaks into the bread just enough to give it a punch of flavor without compromising the texture. It's delicious.

- 4 cups cubed sourdough country white bread (about 4 slices)
- ¼ cup olive oil
- 1 tablespoon red wine vinegar
- 1 teaspoon balsamic vinegar
- 1 clove garlic, crushed through a garlic press
- ¼ teaspoon salt

- ⅛ teaspoon ground black pepper
- 8 cups chopped romaine lettuce
- ½ cup finely chopped fresh basil leaves
- 2 cups chopped fresh tomatoes (about 4 medium)
- 1 cup diced fresh mozzarella (4 ounces; ½-inch dice)

Toast the bread cubes: Heat the oven to 350°F. Spread the bread cubes on a baking sheet and bake until crisp on the outside—5 to 7 minutes. Remove to a wire rack to cool.

Make the salad: In the meantime, to make a dressing, whisk together the oil, vinegars, garlic, salt, and pepper in a small bowl. Place the lettuce in a large salad bowl. Add the basil, tomatoes, mozzarella, and bread cubes. Drizzle with the dressing and toss until the salad is well mixed and evenly coated with dressing. Serve immediately.

Nutrition per serving—Protein: 8.4 G; Fat: 13.9 G; Carbohydrate: 22.7 G; Fiber: 2.8 G; Sodium: 314.2 MG; Cholesterol: 14.9 MG; Calories: 245.

❋ Dessert ❋

dark chocolate butter cake

MAKES 1 TEN-INCH BUNDT CAKE
(ABOUT 16 SERVINGS)

WORKING TIME 20 MINUTES

TOTAL TIME 1 HOUR AND 40 MINUTES

Dutch-processed cocoa, which is especially dark, is a must for this cake—it combines with the strong coffee for a rich, full flavor that gets a subtle accent from a bit of cinnamon. We love this drizzled with raspberry sauce. Shown on page 104.

. . . .

1 cup milk	1 teaspoon ground cinnamon
1 tablespoon white vinegar	1/2 teaspoon baking powder
1 1/2 cups unsalted butter (3 sticks), softened	5 large eggs
2 1/2 cups sugar	2 teaspoons vanilla extract
2 1/4 cups all-purpose flour	1/4 cup brewed espresso or very strong coffee, cooled
3/4 cup Dutch-processed cocoa powder, plus extra for dusting	Raspberry Sauce, for serving (optional, recipe follows)
1 teaspoon salt	Whipped cream, for serving (optional)

DUST WITH COCOA

Cocoa powder works better than flour for dusting chocolate-cake pans, as it doesn't leave a white residue.

Prepare the pan: Heat the oven to 325°F. Butter a 10-inch (10- to 12-cup) Bundt pan well; then dust with cocoa powder, knocking out excess.

Make the batter: Combine the milk and vinegar in a small bowl and set aside to just slightly thicken. Cream the butter and sugar in a large mixing bowl with an electric mixer on high speed, beating for 5 minutes and occasionally scraping down the sides of the bowl. Meanwhile, whisk together the flour, cocoa powder, salt, cinnamon, and baking powder in a medium-size bowl; set aside. Add the eggs one at a time to the butter mixture, beating on high speed after each addition. Beat in the vanilla. Whisk the espresso into the milk mixture by hand. In thirds, alternately add the flour mixture and milk mixture to the butter mixture, beating on medium speed and blending well after each addition.

Bake the cake: Scrape the batter into the prepared pan. Bake until a toothpick inserted in the center comes out clean—65 to 70 minutes. Cool the cake in the pan on a wire rack. Loosen the cake from pan using the tip of a knife, then invert the rack over the pan and turn the cake out onto a cake stand or plate. If you like, drizzle with Raspberry Sauce or top with whipped cream, or use both.

Raspberry Sauce

Heat 2 cups fresh or frozen raspberries, $\frac{1}{3}$ cup sugar, and 1 tablespoon fresh lemon juice in a small saucepan over medium heat until warmed, smashing slightly with a fork to break up the raspberries. Drizzle over the cake before serving. Makes about $1\frac{1}{4}$ cups.

Nutrition per serving without sauce or whipped cream—Protein: 4.8 G; Fat: 21.4 G; Carbohydrate: 47.1 G; Fiber: 0.9 G; Sodium: 193.4 MG; Cholesterol: 113.4 MG; Calories: 380.

Say Yes to New Tools

For years I've made do with what kitchen utensils I had, some so old they were wedding gifts. Recently, I've made an effort to replace worn out utensils and purchase those I was lacking. I didn't even realize that I was missing out on anything until baking with Serena one day: I used her handheld grater to zest a lemon and I was amazed by how effortless it was. It didn't splatter juice and peel all over the place like my 25-year-old grater with the broken handle. That night I started my "wish list." Now as I bake or cook and find myself working with a measuring cup that has a bent handle, or wishing I had longer tongs because the hot oil is splattering on my hands, I pick up a pencil and add it to the list posted on my fridge.

~Teri

coconut cake

MAKES 1 EIGHT-INCH ROUND CAKE (12 TO 16 SERVINGS)
WORKING TIME 40 MINUTES
TOTAL TIME 1 HOUR AND 20 MINUTES

The steps in this cake seem a bit intimidating, but it actually comes together easily. The coconut flavor is subtle and the cake texture is light and fluffy. The white-chocolate frosting and toasted coconut give an extra-special finishing touch.

4 large egg whites

1$2/3$ cups granulated sugar

1 cup unsalted butter (2 sticks), softened

2$1/2$ cups sifted cake flour

1 tablespoon baking powder

$1/2$ teaspoon salt

1$1/4$ cups light unsweetened coconut milk

3 teaspoons coconut flavoring

1 teaspoon vanilla extract

3 ounces white chocolate (3 squares), chopped

4 cups confectioners' sugar

2 cups toasted, unsweetened flaked coconut

Prepare the pans. Heat the oven to 350°F. Lightly coat two 8-inch round cake pans with nonstick cooking oil spray and lightly flour them.

Make the batter: Beat the egg whites in a small bowl with an electric mixer on high speed until soft peaks form. Gradually add $1/3$ cup of the granulated sugar, beating continuously until stiff peaks form; set aside. Wash and dry the beaters. Cream $1/2$ cup (1 stick) of the butter in a medium-size bowl with the mixer on medium speed. Beat in the flour. Sift in the baking powder, salt, and the remaining 1$1/3$ cups granulated sugar, beating until the mixture looks like sand. Shake the can of coconut milk, then open it and add 1 cup to the butter mixture along with 2 teaspoons of the coconut flavoring and the vanilla, beating until combined. Add the egg-white mixture with the mixer on low speed, beating just until combined—do not over beat.

Bake the cake: Divide the batter evenly between the prepared pans. Bake until a wooden toothpick inserted in the center of a cake comes out clean—approximately 20 minutes. Cool in the pans on wire racks for about 5 minutes. Then turn out the cakes onto the racks and cool completely.

Meanwhile, prepare the frosting: Place the white chocolate in a medium-size microwave-safe bowl and microwave on high for 30 seconds; remove and stir. If not completely melted, repeat the microwaving. Add the remaining ¼ cup coconut milk, the remaining 1 teaspoon coconut flavoring, and the confectioners' sugar; beat with clean, dry beaters on medium-high speed until well combined and the chocolate is completely incorporated. Cool to room temperature. Beat in the remaining ½ cup butter (1 stick) until well combined and fluffy.

Assemble the cake: Transfer 1 cake layer to a serving plate. Spread about one-third of the frosting over the top with an offset spatula. Sprinkle ½ cup of the coconut over the frosted layer. Place the second cake layer on the first; spread the remaining frosting over the top and sides and sprinkle the top with the remaining 1½ cups coconut.

Nutrition per smaller serving—Protein: 4 G; Fat: 22.5 G; Carbohydrate: 74.2 G; Fiber: 1.7 G; Sodium: 202.3 MG; Cholesterol: 31.7 MG; Calories: 513.

WHERE TO FIND COCONUT

Look in the Asian foods section of your grocery store for coconut milk. Coconut flavoring will be with the extracts and spices. Unsweetened coconut isn't a common grocery store item, but it can be found in natural food stores.

YO-YO TRIMS

The little cloth circles known as yo-yos were popular during the 1920s, '30s, and '40s. They're quick and easy to make and you don't need a sewing machine, so they're great to carry along to an informal get-together or an appointment where you might have to wait. We think they make a cute trim for this market tote bag, and have used them on clothing too. If you fall in love with them, make lots and sew them together for a coverlet.

4-INCH YO-YO

1. Make a circle template for the yo-yos: Its diameter should be twice the diameter you want the finished yo-yo to be, plus $\frac{1}{2}$ inch for seam allowance. We used a 4-inch diameter template for our yo-yos.

2. Trace the template onto the wrong side of your fabric to mark as many yo-yos as you wish. Cut them out. Fold $\frac{1}{4}$ inch to the wrong side all around each cutout; crease the fold with your fingers or an iron. Thread a hand-sewing needle with thread that matches the fabric; knot the thread. Sew a running stitch around the yo-yo; stitch through the folded margin. Don't cut the thread.

3. Gently pull the thread to gather the edge of the yo-yo—a little pouch will form. Make sure the right side of the fabric is out. Flatten the pouch to make a disk with the gathers in the middle of one side. Take a couple of stitches to secure the gathers and then knot and cut the thread.

4 Arrange the yo-yos as you like on whatever you are embellishing. Sew them in place. We sewed a little button in the center of each yo-yo when we attached ours to this bag.

blackberry crisp

MAKES 1 EIGHT-INCH SQUARE CRISP (ABOUT 9 SERVINGS)

WORKING TIME 20 MINUTES

TOTAL TIME 1 HOUR

For several years of my childhood, we lived on the banks of the Klamath River in Northern California, where blackberries grew like weeds. Our mom would give my siblings and me 5-gallon buckets for picking. We'd spend the day exploring and munching berries, eventually filling the buckets. When we returned, our mom would make tons of blackberry jam and for dessert that night, this blackberry crisp. ~Serena

2 cups fresh blackberries or 1 16-ounce bag frozen blackberries

¾ cup all-purpose flour

¾ cup packed brown sugar

¾ cup old-fashioned rolled oats

½ teaspoon ground cinnamon

½ cup cold unsalted butter (1 stick), cut into small pieces

½ cup chopped walnuts (2 ounces)

Vanilla ice cream, for serving (optional)

Heat the oven to 375°F. Place the blackberries in the bottom of an 8-inch square baking dish. Combine the flour, brown sugar, oats, and cinnamon in a medium-size mixing bowl. Cut the butter into the flour mixture with a pastry cutter or two knives until the mixture forms large crumbs. Stir in the walnuts. Sprinkle the mixture over the berries in the baking dish. Bake until the topping is browned and berries are bubbly—35 to 40 minutes. Serve warm with vanilla ice cream.

Nutrition per serving without ice cream—Protein: 3.5 G; Fat: 15.2 G; Carbohydrate: 34.6 G; Fiber: 3.1 G; Sodium: 7.2 MG; Cholesterol: 27.1 MG; Calories: 280.

FESTIVE SERVING

For a special serving presentation, take clear glass dishes, spoon a bit of warm crisp into the bottom and then top with alternating layers of vanilla ice cream and more crisp. Serve immediately.

apple cake with vanilla or rum sauce

MAKES 1 EIGHT-INCH SQUARE CAKE (ABOUT 9 SERVINGS)
WORKING TIME 20 MINUTES
TOTAL TIME 1 HOUR AND 5 MINUTES

For me, this cake is all about the sauce. I'm partial to the rum version and Serena loves the vanilla. The cake itself has a simple, mellow taste that is perfectly complimented by the cream sauce. It converts well into four mini Bundt pans, perfect for gift giving. And it's easy to make! ~Teri

- 1/4 cup unsalted butter (1/2 stick), softened
- 1 large egg
- 2 tablespoons milk
- 3/4 cup sugar
- 1 cup all-purpose flour
- 1 teaspoon baking soda
- 1/2 teaspoon salt
- 1/2 teaspoon ground nutmeg
- 1/4 teaspoon ground cinnamon
- 2 cups cored, peeled and chopped apples, such as Golden Delicious or Crispin
- 1/2 cup chopped walnuts (2 ounces)
- Vanilla or Rum Sauce (recipe follows)

Heat the oven to 350°F. Butter and flour an 8-inch square cake pan. Cream the butter, egg, milk, and sugar together in a large bowl with an electric mixer on medium speed. Whisk together the flour, baking soda, salt, nutmeg, and cinnamon in a small bowl; then stir into the butter mixture until blended. Stir in the apples and walnuts. Spoon the batter into the prepared pan. Bake until lightly browned and a cake tester inserted in the center comes out clean—40 to 45 minutes. Transfer to a wire rack while you make the sauce. Pour the warm sauce over cake before serving.

Vanilla or Rum Sauce

Melt 1/4 cup unsalted butter (1/2 stick) in a small saucepan over medium heat. Stir in 1/2 cup sugar, 1/4 cup heavy cream, 1/4 teaspoon ground nutmeg, 1/4 teaspoon ground cinnamon, and 1 teaspoon vanilla extract or rum; heat to boiling, stirring constantly. Cook, stirring, about 1 minute more. Remove the pan from the heat and set aside to slightly cool and thicken—5 minutes. Refrigerate any leftover sauce, tightly covered, up to 3 days. Makes about 2/3 cup.

Nutrition per serving with sauce—Protein: 4.3 G; Fat: 17.7 G; Carbohydrate: 43.8 G; Fiber: 1.6 G; Sodium: 282.9 MG; Cholesterol: 60.1 MG; Calories: 342.

SWEET CELEBRATION

This delicious Apple Cake is one of the treats Teri served the day of our son Micah's baptism. Teri and Steve, Micah's godparents, had our extended family over for brunch to celebrate. The brunch was amazing, with so many special little details Teri is known for, like little butter leaves made in small candy molds saved from her wedding reception many years before. ~Serena

make & give
a mini pie

We adore pie and especially love baking our mini versions for gifts. Because pie making is becoming somewhat of a lost art, it seems that people really love receiving a pie, especially one that's been made just for them.

Regular pie recipes can easily be adapted to make mini pies. Generally, a regular pie recipe can be turned into three mini pies, each approximately 4½ inches in diameter. Disposable aluminum mini-pie pans can be found on the baking aisle of most grocery stores. Tin or ceramic versions can be found online or at kitchen specialty shops.

To make a mini pie, follow your recipe as written to prepare the piecrust and filling; then divide the crust and filling equally among three mini-pie pans. Shorten the baking time by about one-quarter to one-third. For example, if the baking time for the regular pie is 50 minutes, shorten the mini-pie baking time to 33 to 37 minutes.

For an extra-special homemade gift, we love packaging our small pies in a special way. We recommend keeping an eye out for unique packaging items while out and about, in order to build up your supplies and have choices readily available whenever you may need to do some gifting. Here are a few of our favorites:

★ Little vintage berry baskets
★ Old tins
★ Mini cake stands
★ Colorful little paper bags, with the top cut off or rolled down

orange meringue pie

MAKES 1 NINE-INCH PIE
(ABOUT 8 SERVINGS)
WORKING TIME 20 MINUTES
TOTAL TIME 30 MINUTES

Pie, not cake, was always my birthday dessert request as a child. Lemon meringue was my favorite. This Orange Meringue Pie is my grown-up adaptation. It's very similar to classic lemon meringue, but in my opinion, even tastier. ~ Serena

. . . .

2 cups sugar

3 tablespoons all-purpose flour

3$\frac{1}{2}$ tablespoons cornstarch

$\frac{1}{4}$ teaspoon salt

$\frac{1}{2}$ cup orange-juice concentrate

3 tablespoons fresh lemon juice

2 tablespoons unsalted butter, cut into pieces

4 large eggs, separated

1 Baked Pie Shell (recipe, page 129)

1 teaspoon vanilla extract

$\frac{1}{2}$ teaspoon cream of tartar

Make the filling: Whisk 1$\frac{1}{2}$ cups of the sugar, the flour, cornstarch, and salt together in a large saucepan. Add the orange-juice concentrate, lemon juice, and 1$\frac{1}{2}$ cups water. Bring the mixture to a boil, whisking continuously. Whisk in the butter, and remove from the heat. Lightly beat the egg yolks in a medium-size bowl; while continuing to whisk, stream in $\frac{1}{2}$ cup of the hot orange-juice mixture. Whisk the yolk mixture into the orange-juice mixture in the saucepan over medium-low heat and continue whisking until very thick and glossy—about 5 minutes. Strain through a fine sieve into the Baked Pie Shell, and set aside.

Make the meringue: Heat the oven to 350°F. Beat the egg whites, vanilla, and cream of tartar to soft peaks using an electric mixer set on medium speed. Continue to beat while adding the remaining $\frac{1}{2}$ cup sugar until stiff peaks form, increasing the mixer speed to high. Gently spread the meringue over the hot filling to the edges of the crust. Use a spoon to make dips and peaks in the meringue. Bake until the meringue is lightly browned—about 10 minutes. Transfer to a wire rack to cool.

Nutrition per serving—Protein: 6.1 G; Fat: 16.9 G; Carbohydrate: 78 G; Fiber: 0.8 G; Sodium: 184 MG; Cholesterol: 143 MG; Calories: 483

cherry crumble pie

MAKES 1 NINE-INCH PIE
(ABOUT 8 SERVINGS)
WORKING TIME 10 MINUTES
TOTAL TIME 55 MINUTES

If you're new to making pies, this is a great recipe to try. The crumb topping is delicious and really a no-fail choice for a top crust. Both our husbands really love this pie.

- 1 29-ounce jar tart pie cherries in water
- ¾ cup granulated sugar
- 3 tablespoons cornstarch
- ½ teaspoon salt
- ⅓ cup all-purpose flour
- ⅓ cup brown sugar
- ⅓ cup old-fashioned rolled oats
- ⅓ cup walnuts, chopped (about 1½ ounces)
- ½ teaspoon ground cinnamon
- 3 tablespoons cold unsalted butter, cut into small pieces
- 1 Baked Pie Shell (recipe, page 129)

Heat the oven to 425°F. Drain the cherries, and reserve ⅓ cup of the liquid. Stir the cherries, granulated sugar, cornstarch, salt, and reserved cherry liquid together in a medium-size bowl. Toss the flour, brown sugar, oats, walnuts, and cinnamon together in another medium-size bowl. Mix in the butter using a pastry blender or your fingers until a crumbly mixture forms. Pour the cherry mixture into the Baked Pie Shell. Sprinkle the crumb topping evenly over the cherries. Bake for 15 minutes. Lower the oven temperature to 350°F and continue to bake until the topping is deep golden brown—30 to 35 minutes more. Transfer to a wire rack to cool slightly. Serve warm.

Nutrition per serving—Protein: 5.1 G; Fat: 19 G; Carbohydrate: 58.6 G; Fiber: 2.3 G; Sodium: 229 MG; Cholesterol: 41 MG; Calories: 417.

butterscotch pie

MAKES 1 NINE-INCH PIE (ABOUT 8 SERVINGS)
WORKING TIME 20 MINUTES
TOTAL TIME 1 HOUR AND 20 MINUTES

This pie reminds us of an amazing dessert you'd find in a huge spinning display of fluffy homemade pies at an undiscovered little roadside café. Old-fashioned, sweet, and generously topped with whipped cream, it's worth a try! Shown on page 120.

½ cup unsalted butter (1 stick)

1¼ cups light-brown sugar

¼ cup cornstarch

3 tablespoons all-purpose flour

½ teaspoon salt

1½ cups cold heavy cream

½ cup milk

4 egg yolks

1 teaspoon vanilla extract

1 Baked Pie Shell (recipe, page 129)

1 teaspoon honey

2 tablespoons confectioners' sugar

Sliced, toasted almonds for sprinkling (optional)

Make the filling: Melt the butter in a medium saucepan over medium heat until it begins to brown. Stir in the brown sugar. Add 1½ cups hot water and whisk until the mixture comes to a boil. Continue to cook for 2 more minutes, remove from the heat, and set aside. Combine the cornstarch, flour, and salt in a small bowl. Whisk in ½ cup each of the cream and milk until smooth; pour into the butter mixture. Whisk continuously over medium heat until the mixture comes to a boil and thickens—about 3 minutes. Remove from the heat. Lightly beat the egg yolks in a medium-size bowl; while continuing to whisk, stream in ½ cup of the hot milk mixture. Whisk the egg mixture into the milk mixture in the saucepan over medium heat for 1 minute. Strain through a fine sieve into a medium-size bowl and stir in the vanilla. Pour into the Baked Pie Shell, and refrigerate until the filling is set.

Make the cream topping: Beat the remaining cup of cream with the honey and confectioners' sugar until stiff peaks form. Spread over the cooled pie and refrigerate until ready to serve. If you wish, sprinkle with sliced, toasted almonds just before serving.

Nutrition per serving without almonds—Protein: 5.3 G; Fat: 42 G; Carbohydrate: 59.3 G; Fiber: 0.7 G; Sodium: 263 MG; Cholesterol: 225 MG; Calories: 629.

STIFF PEAKS

Adding 1 teaspoon of honey to each cup of heavy cream when whipping will stabilize the whipped cream so it doesn't separate if it sits for a while. Add other sweetener as your recipe indicates.

farmhouse apple pie

This is our all-time favorite pie and is probably our most-often used recipe. Our favorite pie apple is Golden Delicious, but any mixture of apples can work just fine. We recommend experimenting with different apple combinations to discover your favorite pie varieties. Shown on page 120.

2 disks Grandma's Pie Dough
(1/2 recipe, page 128)

2 1/2 pounds mixed apples, peeled, cored, and chopped into 3/4-inch pieces

2 tablespoons all-purpose flour

3/4 cup sugar, plus 1 tablespoon

1 teaspoon ground cinnamon

1/4 teaspoon ground nutmeg

1/2 teaspoon salt

1 tablespoon fresh lemon juice

Heat the oven to 375°F. Roll out one of the disks of dough on a lightly floured surface to 1/8-inch thickness; transfer to a 9-inch pie pan. Set aside in the refrigerator. Roll the remaining dough to 1/8-inch thickness. Set aside on a parchment paper-lined baking sheet in the refrigerator. Toss the chopped apples, flour, 3/4 cup sugar, cinnamon, nutmeg, salt, and lemon juice together and mix until combined. Pour the apple mixture into the prepared pie pan and top with the remaining dough. Trim, leaving a 1/2-inch overhang; fold under and crimp the edges. Sprinkle the top with the remaining tablespoon of sugar; chill for 10 minutes. Bake until the fruit is bubbling and the crust is golden brown—50 to 55 minutes. Transfer to a wire rack to cool.

Nutrition per serving—Protein: 4.5 G; Fat: 21 G; Carbohydrate: 65.7 G; Fiber: 2.9 G; Sodium: 264 MG; Cholesterol: 68 MG; Calories: 456

APPLE PREP

When cutting apples for pie, we peel and core each apple and then cut them into quarters. We cut each quarter in half, lengthwise, and then thinly chop into bite-sized pieces. Each bite of pie is easily cut into with a fork, which we think makes it just a little more special.

perfect
piecrust

A delicious, flaky, beautiful golden-brown crust is the signature of a really great pie. While for many bakers the thought of making a crust from scratch is daunting, it really needn't be.

Six tips for piecrust success:
1. Follow directions carefully.
2. Use cold butter and water.
3. Once the liquid has been added, don't overwork the dough.
4. For easier handling, chill the dough before rolling it out.
5. To transfer the crust to the pie pan, roll it up on your rolling pin, then unroll over the pan.
6. To keep the edge of the crust from over-browning and getting hard, tuck a narrow piece of foil around the crimped edge only. Remove the foil during the final 15 minutes of baking to allow the crust to brown. There are piecrust shields on the market, but foil works just as well.

Your first pie may not be the perfect pie, but that's okay. It will still be delicious, and after a few tries, you'll get the hang of making a crust that looks as good as it tastes.

Top: Farmhouse Apple Pie, page 119; bottom: Butterscotch Pie, page 118.

TERI'S 3-STEP LATTICE TOP CRUST

It's as easy as pie to make a lattice top crust like the one we use for the Peach Huckleberry pie on page 123. If you'd like wavy edges on the lattice strips, use a pastry wheel to cut them. Begin with prepared dough for two crusts (half of Grandma's Pie Dough recipe on page 128).

1. Roll out the dough for the bottom crust and fit it into the pie pan so it overhangs the edge. Roll out the remaining dough into an oblong. Cut 8 to 10 half-inch-wide strips of pastry using a sharp knife or pastry wheel. Add your filing to the bottom crust in the pie pan.

2. Starting at one edge of the pie, lay half the strips lengthwise over the filling, spacing them evenly. Gently bend back alternate strips and lay a strip crosswise over the ones remaining flat. Lay the bent strips flat again and bend back the ones in between them. Lay another strip crosswise over the flat strips.

3. Continue to bend back alternate strips and weave the over-under lattice. When all the strips are in position, trim any long ends, fold up the bottom crust over the strips, and crimp the edge to seal. Bake the pie according to your recipe directions.

peach huckleberry lattice pie

MAKES	1 NINE-INCH PIE (ABOUT 8 SERVINGS)
WORKING TIME	25 MINUTES
TOTAL TIME	1 HOUR AND 25 MINUTES

We're lucky that huckleberries grow wild just a short drive from our homes, on Mt. Spokane. One of my daughter Kate's favorite huckleberry memories is of Serena, pregnant with her third son, Lucas, packing second son, Micah, on her back, with an empty milk jug for holding huckleberries strapped to her belt, picking away! ~Teri

2 disks Grandma's Pie Dough
(½ recipe, page 128)

5 cups 1-inch slices fresh peaches
(about 5 medium)

½ cup fresh huckleberries or blueberries

¾ cup sugar

4 tablespoons all-purpose flour

½ teaspoon ground cinnamon

Prepare the dough and lattice strips: Heat the oven to 400°F. Roll out one of the disks of dough on a lightly floured surface to ⅛-inch thickness; transfer to a 9-inch pie pan and trim, leaving a ½-inch overhang. Set aside in the refrigerator. Roll the remaining disk of dough to ⅛-inch thickness, making a rectangle about 10 by 13 inches. Cut 10 one-inch-wide strips using a pizza wheel or fluted pastry cutter. Lay the strips on a parchment paper-lined baking sheet, cover with plastic wrap, and refrigerate until ready to use.

Make the pie: Toss the peaches, huckleberries, sugar, flour, and cinnamon together in a large bowl. Pour the filling into the prepared pie pan. Lay 5 of the pastry strips on top, spacing about 1 inch apart; then weave the lattice top with the remaining 5 strips (see Teri's 3-Step Lattice Top Crust method, page 121). Trim the strip ends even with the bottom crust overhang. Fold the bottom crust over the lattice strips and crimp together. Refrigerate for 10 minutes. Bake until the fruit is bubbling and the crust is golden brown—50 to 55 minutes. Transfer to a wire rack to cool.

Nutrition per serving—Protein: 4.9 G; Fat: 21 G; Carbohydrate: 58.6 G; Fiber: 2.9 G; Sodium: 118 MG; Cholesterol: 68 MG; Calories: 432.

BERRY TIP

Wild huckleberries are plentiful high in the mountains of the Pacific Northwest. They're similar to the blueberry, just a little bit tarter and much smaller. Unfortunately, cultivated bushes are not available. You can find sources for purchasing the berries online.

Making Old New

· · · · · · · · · · · · · ·

We both collect colorful vintage tablecloths and often find what we call "cutters"—pieces that have holes or irremovable stains, yet still have plenty of usable fabric that isn't damaged. Since the "cutters" tend to be inexpensive, we have accumulated quite a collection and use them for various projects, such as these dishtowels. The beauty of the old tablecloths is that they're made from really great cotton or linen and are so absorbent and durable.

We usually buy stained tablecloths in person at thrift shops and yard and estate sales, but shy away from "cutter" tablecloths that we find in online auctions, as it's really hard to determine the actual condition of "cutters" online. To remove the stains, we've had good luck soaking the tablecloths for several hours in hot water with OxiClean, which you can find at most groceries.

~ Serena

THE FARM CHICKS

EMBELLISHED DISHTOWELS

The bias tape makers are readily available, inexpensive, simple to use, and come in many different sizes. The finished bias tape is single fold (meaning the two long edges are folded over to meet in the center), so you'll need to fold it in half and press it to make it double fold (ready to encase the edge of the towel). We like using ¼-inch bias tape for this project, which means you'll need to use a ½-inch tape maker, as you'll be folding the tape in half.

1. Using a favorite dishtowel as a guide for size, cut out a tablecloth piece for each towel you wish to make.

2. Following the directions on the package of the bias tape maker, make as much bias tape as needed to go all the way around each towel, plus a little extra for turning under at the corners. Fold the finished bias tape in half lengthwise (with the cut edges on the inside) and gently press the fold with your iron.

3. Slip the folded bias tape over the raw edges of each dishtowel, folding neatly at the corners. Pin or baste, and topstitch into place through all layers.

Bias tape is a favorite crafting material of ours, making sewn projects much easier while adding a great finishing touch. On a trip to our local fabric shop, we discovered bias tape makers, which sent us over the moon thinking about the possibilities. One idea we really love is to add colorful binding to the edges of dishtowels cut from vintage tablecloths. We've gone crazy making bias tape using darling patterned fabric.

strawberry rhubarb pie

MAKES 1 NINE-INCH PIE (ABOUT 8 SERVINGS)	
WORKING TIME 20 MINUTES	
TOTAL TIME 1 HOUR AND 15 MINUTES	

The sweetness of strawberries balanced with the tartness of rhubarb makes this a delicious sweet-and-sour pie. When the delicate pink syrupy filling is revealed, it's hard to resist. This pie is best in spring and early summer when rhubarb is abundant and strawberries can be picked right off the vine.

2 disks Grandma's Pie Dough ($1/2$ recipe, page 128)

$1^1/3$ pounds rhubarb, cut into 1-inch pieces (about $4^1/2$ cups)

$1/3$ pound strawberries, hulled and halved (about 1 cup)

$3/4$ cup sugar

$1/3$ cup all-purpose flour

Heat the oven to 375°F. Roll out one disk of dough on a lightly floured surface to $1/8$-inch thickness, and transfer to a 9-inch pie pan. Set aside in the refrigerator. Roll the remaining dough to $1/8$-inch thickness and use a miniature star cutter to pierce it, as shown, or a sharp knife to cut slits in it. Combine the rhubarb, strawberries, sugar, and flour in a large bowl, and transfer to the prepared pie pan; drape the pierced rolled-out dough over the pie. Trim the edges of both crusts, leaving a $1/2$-inch overhang. Fold the dough under, lightly pinching to seal. Crimp around the rim and refrigerate for 10 minutes. Bake on the center shelf of the oven until the crust is golden brown—45 to 55 minutes. Transfer to a wire rack to cool.

Nutrition per serving—Protein: 5.2 G; Fat: 21 G; Carbohydrate: 52.6 G; Fiber: 2.6 G; Sodium: 121 MG; Cholesterol: 68 MG; Calories: 412.

GROW YOUR OWN

Rhubarb plants are incredibly easy to grow and are drought resistant. Your friends may have some to divide and give away, or you can buy them at your local nursery.

A farmer friend of ours, Verne, from Strawberry Hill Farm, harvests rhubarb beginning in the spring and continually through the end of summer. His trick is mowing his plants down a few times throughout the season. The plants regenerate themselves, putting out whole new bunches of shoots each time.

grandma's pie dough

MAKES 4 SINGLE CRUSTS
WORKING TIME 10 MINUTES
TOTAL TIME 1 HOUR AND 10 MINUTES

You can't judge a book by its cover, but you can judge a pie by its crust. This is hands-down the best piecrust ever, adapted from my mother-in-law Mary Jane's recipe. It's rich, flaky and unforgettable. You can make the dough, wrap it, and freeze for baking later. ~Serena

- 4 cups all-purpose flour
- ¾ teaspoon salt
- 1 tablespoon sugar
- 1¾ cups cold unsalted butter (3½ sticks), cut into small pieces
- 1 tablespoon white vinegar
- 1 extra-large egg

Combine the flour, salt, and sugar in a large bowl. Cut in the butter using a pastry blender or your fingers until the mixture resembles coarse meal. Whisk the vinegar, egg, and ½ cup of ice water together and mix into the flour mixture with your hands until just combined. Transfer to a clean work surface, and gently press to form a dough. Divide the dough into 4 equal parts. Shape each into a ball, flatten slightly to form a disk, and wrap in plastic. Chill for at least 1 hour. Roll out as indicated in your recipe.

Nutrition per one-half single crust—Protein: 2 G; Fat: 10 G; Carbohydrate: 12.7 G; Fiber: 0.4 G; Sodium: 59 MG; Cholesterol: 34 MG; Calories: 150.

FAMILY HISTORY

Mary Jane was given the original version of this recipe by a friend while living in San Diego and adjusting to life as a new mom with a husband at war. I often think of her when preparing this dough and can only imagine what a challenging time it must have been for her. Yet somehow, she still made time to bake pies. I love that. ~Serena

baked pie shell

The classic piecrust, essential for a great pie. We recommend using this recipe for all single crust pies, as the high butter content in our Grandma's Pie Dough recipe (on the facing page) causes single crusts to shrink when baked.

. . . .

1¼ cups all-purpose flour

¼ teaspoon salt

½ cup cold unsalted butter (1 stick),
  cut into small pieces

Make the dough: Combine the flour and salt in a large bowl. Cut in the butter using a pastry blender or your fingers until the mixture resembles coarse meal. Sprinkle 4 to 6 tablespoons of ice water over the flour mixture and mix with your hands until just combined. Transfer the mixture to a clean work surface, and gently press together until a dough begins to form. Gather into a ball and flatten slightly to form a disk. Wrap in plastic; chill for at least 1 hour.

Bake the shell: Heat the oven to 450°F. Roll out the dough on a lightly floured surface to ⅛-inch thickness. Transfer to a 9-inch pie pan and trim, leaving a ½-inch overhang. Fold the ½-inch excess under and crimp along the rim using a fork or your fingers. Prick the bottom and sides of the dough with a fork. Bake on the center shelf of the oven until lightly browned—10 to 12 minutes. Cool completely on a wire rack before filling as indicated in your recipe.

Nutrition per one-half single crust—Protein: 2.1 G; Fat: 12 G; Carbohydrate: 15 G; Fiber: 0.5 G; Sodium: 75 MG; Cholesterol: 30 MG; Calories: 171.

FLOYD AND MARGARET

Our lives have been touched by the families we have met while traveling the back roads of our region. Many of them live simply, without expensive possessions. We've found that their loved ones are the most important thing of all, and that less can sometimes mean more. These families continue to inspire us, for nothing we do would be meaningful without our families to share it with. And sometimes, if we're lucky, we see a real-life love story. Floyd and Margaret are just that.

We first met Floyd when we stopped by his farm to inquire about his enormous junkyard on the back side of his property. He was walking up the dirt road to his house from the lower pasture where he'd been tending to his cattle. His old flannel shirt was worn and dotted with scrap patches that had been meticulously hand-stitched into place. His face was deeply creased, almost scowl-like, and his eyes were dark and full of wisdom. His voice was gruff when he spoke, contradicting the small bouquet of wildflowers he was carrying, which he had just picked for his wife, Margaret.

Margaret stood with eyes twinkling and beamed as Floyd handed her the flowers. In seeing her reaction, Floyd's face erupted in an ear-to-ear grin, erasing the years of hard work reflected in his face. He told us that he always picked flowers for Margaret and said he felt like they were married just yesterday. He grinned boastfully and asked, "How old do you think she is? Isn't she beautiful?" Floyd bragged that he felt like he was 18 years old and attributed that to 80-something years of "no booze, one woman, and the love of God." Needless to say, we've learned a lot from Floyd and Margaret, a lot in part just by watching the two of them interact.

We've purchased truckloads of old goods and salvage from their property over the years, and on every occasion, Floyd is as ornery as ever. He doesn't like to part with anything that could be of future use on the farm and likes to know what we'll do with the items we buy.

One of his favorites is the necklaces we've made from his vintage wallpaper. On one occasion, we found a pile of license plates, and Teri was interested in one that was from our neighboring state of Idaho. He set a high price, explaining that license plates were useful and that he could do something with them someday. He gruffly asked her what she wanted it for. She told him it bore the year of her birth and that she'd hang it on a wall in her house. He looked at her, smiled, and the price went down.

Recently, Floyd has found it difficult to mow the lawn on his own. In true-love fashion, he and Margaret now push the lawnmower together.

We've delighted in Margaret's Special Oatmeal Cookies, which Floyd says can't be duplicated by anyone. "There's just something she does to make them so good" he says. We've made the cookies and love her recipe, but agree with Floyd. They are even more special in Margaret's kitchen. Try them; see what you think.

margaret's special oatmeal cookies

- 2 cups all-purpose flour
- 2 cups old-fashioned rolled oats
- 1 teaspoon baking soda
- 1 teaspoon cinnamon (Margaret uses apple pie spice)
- ½ teaspoon salt
- 1 cup unsalted butter (2 sticks) (Margaret uses margarine)
- ¾ cup packed light-brown sugar
- 2 large eggs
- 1 teaspoon vanilla extract

Mix the batter: Heat the oven to 350°F. Whisk together the flour, rolled oats, baking soda, cinnamon, and salt in a medium-size bowl. Cream the butter and brown sugar in a large bowl with an electric mixer on medium speed. Beat in the eggs and vanilla. Gradually add the flour mixture to the butter mixture, beating on low speed just until well combined.

Bake the cookies: Drop the batter by tablespoonfuls onto a baking sheet, spacing about 2 inches apart. Bake the cookies just until lightly browned on the bottom and the tops are set—9 to 11 minutes. Don't overcook, or they won't be soft. Let the cookies sit on the baking sheet for 1 minute, then transfer them to a wire rack to cool. Store in an airtight container.

MAKES 30 THREE-INCH COOKIES

Nutrition per cookie—Protein: 2 G; Fat: 7 G; Carbohydrate: 15.5 G; Fiber: 0.8 G; Sodium: 87.9 MG; Cholesterol: 30.4 MG; Calories: 131.

peppermint patties

MAKES 24 TWO-INCH FILLED COOKIES
WORKING TIME 50 MINUTES
TOTAL TIME 2 HOURS

These cookies are the perfect balance of peppermint and chocolate—they're completely addictive. For an extra-special treat, chill them in the refrigerator and serve cold.

. . . .

14 tablespoons unsalted butter, softened

1/4 cup granulated sugar

1/4 cup packed light-brown sugar

1 large egg yolk

1 teaspoon vanilla extract

1 cup all-purpose flour, plus 2 tablespoons

1/4 cup Dutch-processed cocoa powder

1/4 teaspoon salt

1 cup confectioners' sugar

1 1/2 teaspoons peppermint extract

1 teaspoon milk or light cream

2 cups milk chocolate chips

Prepare the dough: Cream 10 tablespoons of the butter in a large bowl with an electric mixer on medium speed. Add the granulated and brown sugars and beat until fluffy. Beat in the egg yolk and vanilla. Add the flour, cocoa powder, and salt with the mixer on low speed, beating until combined. The mixture will seem dry at first, but will come together after a few minutes. Roll the dough into a 10- by 2-inch log; wrap in plastic wrap and refrigerate for 1 hour.

Bake the cookies: Heat the oven to 375°F. Cut the dough into 1/4-inch slices. Place 1 inch apart on a baking sheet (they will not spread). Bake until just firm to the touch—7 to 8 minutes. Transfer the cookies from the baking sheet to a wire rack to cool (these break if you let them cool on the sheets).

Fill the cookies: Cream the remaining 4 tablespoons butter, the confectioners' sugar, peppermint extract, and milk in a small bowl with the mixer on medium speed until blended. Sandwich the cooled cookies together with the filling. Place the chocolate chips in a small microwave-safe bowl and microwave on medium-high for 30 seconds (milk chocolate is sensitive to high heat); remove and stir. If not completely melted, repeat the microwaving. Dip half of each cookie in the melted chocolate and place on a sheet of parchment paper or wax paper until the chocolate is firm.

Nutrition per cookie—Protein: 2 G; Fat: 11.6 G; Carbohydrate: 22.5 G; Fiber: 0.7 G; Sodium: 37.5 MG; Cholesterol: 29.8 MG; Calories: 197.

Peppermint Patties shown opposite (lower right), with Lemon Tea Cookies, page 134.

lemon tea cookies

MAKES FORTY-EIGHT 1½-INCH COOKIES
WORKING TIME 15 MINUTES
TOTAL TIME 2 HOURS

We call these tea cookies because they're perfect for just that. Imagine serving these, along with some flavorful tea, on a special afternoon with your dearest friends. These dainty little cookies just melt in your mouth. Shown on page 133.

1½ cups all-purpose flour

½ cup cornstarch

⅓ cup confectioners' sugar, sifted

⅛ teaspoon salt

¾ cup unsalted butter (1½ sticks), softened

2 tablespoons fresh lemon juice

2 teaspoons grated lemon zest

Lemon Frosting (recipe follows)

Make the dough: Whisk together the flour, cornstarch, confectioners' sugar, and salt in a medium-size bowl. Cream the butter in a large bowl with an electric mixer on medium speed; add the lemon juice and zest, beating until combined. Add the flour mixture to the butter mixture and beat on low speed until well combined.

Shape the dough: Divide dough in half. Roll each half into a log approximately 1½ by 8 inches. Wrap in plastic wrap and refrigerate for 1 hour.

Bake the cookies: Heat the oven to 350°F. Cut each dough log into ¼-inch slices; arrange on baking sheets, spacing about 1-inch apart. Bake until cookies are firm—10 to 12 minutes. Transfer the cookies from the baking sheets to a wire rack to cool. Spread Lemon Frosting over each cookie.

Lemon Frosting

Beat 1 cup sifted confectioners' sugar, ¼ cup softened unsalted butter, and 2 teaspoons fresh lemon juice in a medium-size bowl with an electric mixer on medium-high speed until light and fluffy. Use immediately. Makes about ½ cup.

Nutrition per cookie—Protein: 0.4 G; Fat: 2.9 G; Carbohydrate: 7.6 G; Fiber: 0.1 G; Sodium: 6.8 MG; Cholesterol: 7.6 MG; Calories: 58.

pecan chocolate chip shortbread

MAKES TWENTY-FOUR 4½ INCH COOKIES
WORKING TIME 20 MINUTES
TOTAL TIME 40 MINUTES

This is my all-time favorite cookie! I've always loved the crunchy texture of shortbread, and with the addition of ground pecans and mini chocolate chips, this version is especially flavorful and perfect to enjoy with a cup of coffee! ~Teri

1¾ cups all-purpose flour

¼ teaspoon salt

⅓ cup ground or finely chopped pecans (about 1¼ ounces)

¾ cup unsalted butter (1½ sticks), softened

½ cup sugar

2 teaspoons vanilla extract

¾ cup mini chocolate chips

Make the dough: Heat the oven to 350°F. Generously butter two 9-inch pie pans. Combine the flour, salt and pecans in a small bowl. Cream the butter and sugar together in a large bowl with an electric mixer on medium speed. Beat in the vanilla. Gradually add the flour mixture. Stir in the chocolate chips.

Bake the shortbread: Divide the dough in half and press each portion into a prepared pan, patting smooth with your fingers. Score the dough in each pan into 12 small wedges, cutting halfway through with a paring knife. Bake until lightly browned—18 to 20 minutes. Transfer the pans to wire racks. When cool, cut the shortbreads into wedges along the scored lines and then remove from the pans.

Nutrition per shortbread—Protein: 1.4 G; Fat: 8.5 G; Carbohydrate: 14.8 G; Fiber: 0.7 G; Sodium: 25.8 MG; Cholesterol: 15.3 MG; Calories: 137.

vintage
vases

To prevent damage to your vintage objects, use a glass or plastic container to hold the water. Canning jars and recycled glass food jars work really well.

For shallow vases, use water-soaked floral foam to help hold heavy flowers' stems in place.

*F*lowers bring us so much joy. Whether you grow and pick them yourself or buy them at your local market, displaying in fun creative ways will make even the simplest bouquet shine. To make an extra special gift, find a darling container and fill it with your friend's favorite flowers. Long after the flowers are gone, your friend will be reminded of your thoughtfulness.

One of our favorite ways to display flowers is using objects that we find around our homes, such as:

★ Old thermoses and coolers
★ Vintage graphic metal trash cans
★ Cute old tins
★ Vintage wicker purses
★ Old dairy cartons
★ Toy trucks
★ Vintage working man's metal lunch boxes

✳ spicy camp bars

MAKES EIGHTEEN 3- BY 4¼-INCH BARS
WORKING TIME 15 MINUTES
TOTAL TIME 45 MINUTES

My mom always made these when we went on camping trips. Of course with six kids, she would double the batch and I'm sure they still didn't last long. When I bake these, that sweet, spicy smell always brings back some of my favorite childhood memories. ~Teri

GOOD AS COOKIES TOO

These bars can just as easily be made as cookies. Heat the oven to 375°F. Drop the batter by rounded tablespoonfuls onto a baking sheet and bake for approximately 10 to 13 minutes. The spices give these a golden brown look even when they're not fully cooked, so to see if they're done, lightly touch the center of a cookie—it should have a little give. Remember, cookies continue to bake on the sheet after they're removed from the oven; for chewier cookies, remove these from the sheet immediately, or leave them to cool on the sheet for crisper cookies.

2¼ cups all-purpose flour

2 teaspoons ground cinnamon

1 teaspoon baking soda

½ teaspoon salt

½ teaspoon ground cloves

½ teaspoon ground nutmeg

¾ cup unsalted butter (1½ sticks), softened

¾ cup packed light-brown sugar

¾ cup granulated sugar

1 teaspoon vanilla extract

2 large eggs

1 cup semisweet chocolate chips

Heat the oven to 350°F. Whisk together the flour, cinnamon, baking soda, salt, cloves, and nutmeg in a medium-size bowl. Cream the butter in a large bowl with an electric mixer set on medium speed; beat in the brown and granulated sugars and vanilla until creamy. Add the eggs to the butter mixture, beating until combined. Gradually add the flour mixture, beating until smooth. Stir in the chocolate chips. Press the batter into a 13- by 9-inch baking pan. Bake until golden brown—25 to 30 minutes. Cool in the pan on a wire rack. Cut into 18 bars, approximately 3- by 4¼-inches each.

Nutrition per bar—Protein: 2.8 G; Fat: 11.2 G; Carbohydrate: 35.6 G; Fiber: 1.2 G; Sodium: 147.5 MG; Cholesterol: 43.9 MG; Calories: 247.

big & chewy peanut butter cookies

MAKES ABOUT 20 FIVE-INCH COOKIES
WORKING TIME 20 MINUTES
TOTAL TIME 55 MINUTES

These are my son Ethan's favorite cookies. They're extra peanut buttery in flavor, accented by a hint of honey, and perfect for those who prefer a big, chewy peanut butter cookie over a crunchy one. I personally love the dough! ~Serena

- 1 cup unsalted butter (2 sticks), softened
- 1 cup packed brown sugar
- 1 cup crunchy peanut butter
- ½ cup honey
- 2 teaspoons vanilla extract

- 2 large eggs
- 2 cups all-purpose flour
- 1 cup whole-wheat flour
- 1 teaspoon baking soda
- ¼ teaspoon salt
- 1 cup salted peanuts, for topping (optional)

Make the batter: Heat the oven to 375°F. Cream the butter in a large bowl with an electric mixer on medium speed. Beat in the brown sugar, peanut butter, honey, vanilla, and eggs, mixing until well combined. Stir in the all-purpose and whole-wheat flours, baking soda, and salt with a wooden spoon, stirring until completely incorporated.

Bake the cookies: Drop the batter by ¼-cupfuls onto baking sheets, spacing about 3 inches apart. If you like, press at least 4 peanuts into the top of each cookie, or press a crosshatch pattern into each with the tines of a fork. Bake until lightly browned—12 to 15 minutes. Transfer the cookies from the baking sheets to a wire rack to cool. The cookies will appear slightly undercooked in the center, but will firm up once they've cooled. Store in an airtight container.

Nutrition per cookie without peanuts—Protein: 6 G; Fat: 16.3 G; Carbohydrate: 34.5 G; Fiber: 2.1 G; Sodium: 166.5 MG; Cholesterol: 45.6 MG; Calories: 299.

TABLETOP COVERING

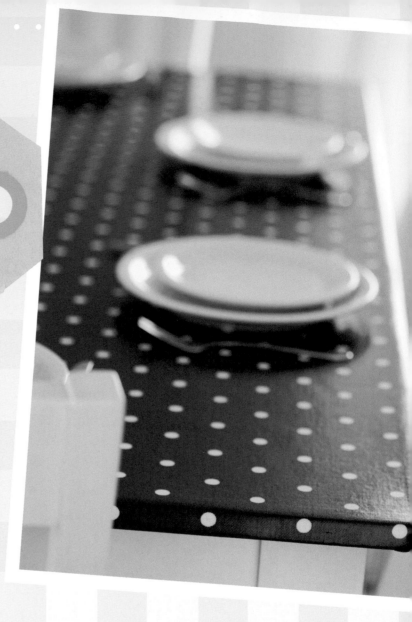

Shortly after Colin and I were married, we purchased our dining room table. It has served our family well over the years, but the top was beginning to look really worn and scratched up. I considered sanding it down and refinishing it but really didn't want to embark on another time-consuming project. After seeing an old linoleum-covered dresser at an estate sale, I was inspired to cover our table and figured oilcloth would be the easiest, most flexible solution. I love how it turned out. We can still use a regular tablecloth over the top whenever we'd like a little bit of a change. Of course, when we tire of the current oilcloth pattern, we can easily change it to another.

~Serena

1. Spread the oilcloth over the top of the table, right side up. Using the table contour as a guide, make sure the pattern is centered nicely; weight the cloth with bowls or books to keep it in position.

2. Cut the oilcloth to size, allowing an overhang on all edges that is long enough wrap around the edge and staple to the underside of the tabletop. The overhang was approximately 2 inches for the table in the photo.

Today's Oilcloth

Originally oilcloth was made from a natural fiber that was treated with a linseed oil solution to make it waterproof. It was available by the foot at many "five-and-dime" stores. It was economical and durable, making it a common tabletop or work surface covering in the kitchen. It went out of style in the late 1950s as the flannel-backed vinyl tablecloths came on the market. We've never been lucky enough to find a use-able piece of vintage oilcloth as it's usually well worn and brittle. Fabric stores carry a variety of the modern oilcloth alternative, which is vinyl-coated cotton fabric, but we've found there's a better variety of colors and styles at online international or auction sites.

~Teri

3. Using a hand held heavy-duty staple gun, attach the oil-cloth to the underside of the tabletop. First staple the middle of 2 opposite sides, then the middle of the remaining opposite sides, pulling the cloth taut. Continue all around the tabletop, pulling the cloth taut while making sure the pattern remains straight and even.

GOOD SCRAPS

You'll find tons of uses for this durable cloth. Save the scraps for our countertop utensil project (page 81) or for another project you come up with.

Metric Equivalent Charts

The recipes in this book use the standard United States method for measuring liquid and dry or solid ingredients (teaspoons, tablespoons, and cups). The information on this chart is provided to help cooks outside the U.S. successfully use these recipes. All equivalents are approximate.

METRIC EQUIVALENTS FOR DIFFERENT TYPES OF INGREDIENTS

A standard cup measure of a dry or solid ingredient will vary in weight depending on the type of ingredient. A standard cup of liquid is the same volume for any type of liquid. Use the following chart when converting standard cup measures to grams (weight) or milliliters (volume).

STANDARD CUP	FINE POWDER (E.G., FLOUR)	GRAIN (E.G., RICE)	GRANULAR (E.G., SUGAR)	LIQUID SOLIDS (E.G., BUTTER)	LIQUID (E.G., MILK)
1	140 g	150 g	190 g	200 g	240 ml
¾	105 g	113 g	143 g	150 g	180 ml
⅔	93 g	100 g	125 g	133 g	160 ml
½	70 g	75 g	95 g	100 g	120 ml
⅓	47 g	50 g	63 g	67 g	80 ml
¼	35 g	38 g	48 g	50 g	60 ml
⅛	18 g	19 g	24 g	25 g	30 ml

USEFUL EQUIVALENTS FOR LIQUID INGREDIENTS BY VOLUME

¼ tsp	=					1 ml
½ tsp	=					2 ml
1 tsp	=					5 ml
3 tsp	=	1 tblsp	=	½ fl oz	=	15 ml
		2 tblsp	= ⅛ cup	1 fl oz	=	30 ml
		4 tblsp	= ¼ cup	2 fl oz	=	60 ml
		5⅓ tblsp	= ⅓ cup	3 fl oz	=	80 ml
		8 tblsp	= ½ cup	4 fl oz	=	120 ml
		10⅔ tblsp	= ⅔ cup	5 fl oz	=	160 ml
		12 tblsp	= ¾ cup	6 fl oz	=	180 ml
		16 tblsp	= 1 cup	8 fl oz	=	240 ml
		1 pt	= 2 cups	16 fl oz	=	480 ml
		1 qt	= 4 cups	32 fl oz	=	960 ml
				33 fl oz	=	1000 ml = 1 l

USEFUL EQUIVALENTS FOR DRY INGREDIENTS BY WEIGHT
(To convert ounces to grams, multiply the number of ounces by 30.)

1 oz	=	1/16 lb	=	30 g
4 oz	=	¼ lb	=	120 g
8 oz	=	½ lb	=	240 g
12 oz	=	¾ lb	=	360 g
16 oz	=	1 lb	=	480 g

USEFUL EQUIVALENTS FOR COOKING/OVEN TEMPERATURES

	Farenheit	Celcius	Gas Mark
Freeze Water	32° F	0° C	
Room Temperature	68° F	20° C	
Boil Water	212° F	100° C	
Bake	325° F	160° C	3
	350° F	180° C	4
	375° F	190° C	5
	400° F	200° C	6
	425° F	220° C	7
	450° F	23° C	8
Broil			Grill

USEFUL EQUIVALENTS FOR LENGTH
(To convert inches to centimeters, multiply the number of inches by 2.5.)

1 in	=					2.5 cm		
6 in	=	½ ft	=			15 cm		
12 in	=	1 ft	=			30 cm		
36 in	=	3 ft	=	1 yd	=	90 cm		
40 in	=					100 cm	=	1 m

Index

······